BEYOND
—DIFFERENCES—

HOW GREAT LEADERS BUILD BRIDGES,
DRIVE CHANGE, AND SUSTAIN IMPACT

T. RENEE' SMITH

Beyond Differences: How Great Leaders Build Bridges, Drive Change, and Sustain Impact

Copyright © 2024 T. Reneé Smith

All Rights Reserved. Published 2024

ISBN-13: 978-1-7331858-7-5

All rights reserved. Printed in the United States of America.

Contents and/or cover may not be reproduced in whole or in part in any form without expressed written consent from the author.

Every effort has been made to make this book as complete and accurate as possible. However, there may be errors, both typographical and in content. Therefore, the information contained herein should be used as a general guide, and not as the ultimate source of educating oneself personally or professionally. The opinions expressed in this book are solely the opinions of the author. The author shall have neither liability nor responsibility to any person or entity with respect to any loss or damage caused, or alleged to have been caused, directly or indirectly, by the material in this book.

Printed in the United States of America

T. Reneé Smith
c/o iSuccess Consulting, Inc.
5829 Campbellton Road, SW
Suite 104-205
Atlanta, Georgia 30331
www.isuccessconsulting.com

TABLE OF CONTENTS

PREFACE 1
INTRODUCTION 3
    The Origin of this Book 4
    The Depth of Diversity 5
    But You Ask, What's in It for Me? 6
    Before You Begin 9

CHAPTER 1: EVOLUTION OF DIVERSITY 11
    In This Chapter: 11
    A Historian's Perspective 12
    History's Impact on DEI 15
        Historical Diversity 16
    The Systemic Racism Conversation 18
        Social Capital Contributions 19
    A Timeline of DEI Relating to Corporate Initiatives 23
    Redefining Diversity 27
    Four Types of Diversity 30
    Reflection and Application 32

CHAPTER 2: WHY DIVERSITY MATTERS 33
    In This Chapter 33
    Business Case for DEIB 34
    Results of Properly Implementing DEIB 37
    DEIB is a Competitive Edge 39
    Why Most DEIB Initiatives Fail 42
        Lack of Transparency and Trust 43

  Lack of Support 44
  Lack of Action 46
 MYTHS AND MISCONCEPTIONS 48
 BARRIERS TO DEIB 56
 OVERCOMING BARRIERS 59
 DEIB BEST PRACTICES 61
  Engage and Ask 63
  Attract and Recruit 64
  Onboarding 66
  Employee Investment 69
  Supplier Based Diversity (SBD) 72
  The DEIB Expert 73
 REFLECTION AND APPLICATION 76

CHAPTER 3: GETTING BUY-IN & COMMITMENT AT ALL LEVELS 77
 IN THIS CHAPTER 77
 C-SUITE EXECUTIVES AND BOARD OF DIRECTORS 79
  How C-Suite Executives Can Promote DEIB at Work 84
  Involvement of the Board of Directors in DEIB initiatives 86
 DEIB COMMITTEE OR COUNCIL 91
 PEOPLE LEADERS 93
 EMPLOYEE RESOURCE GROUPS 96
 EMPLOYEE BUY-IN 98
 EXTERNAL STAKEHOLDERS 99
 REFLECTION AND APPLICATION 100

CHAPTER 4: THE DEIB QUADRANT™ 101
 IN THIS CHAPTER 101
 THE DEIB JOURNEY 102
 ASK QUESTIONS 103
 THE SLIDING SCALE AND COURAGE 104
 START BY ADDRESSING THE STATUS QUO FOR
 COMMON GROUND 105
 THE SIX PS AND THE DEIB QUADRANT 106
 REFLECTION AND APPLICATION 110

CHAPTER 5: TWO SIDES OF THE DEIB STORY 111
 IN THIS CHAPTER 111
 PERFORMING THE DEIB AUDIT 113

Best Survey Questions for a DEIB Audit 114
Analyzing the Data 115
Reflection and Application 117

CHAPTER 6: DEVELOPING YOUR DEIB ROADMAP 119
In This Chapter 119
Preparation 120
Development 122
Implementation 123
Review and Refine 125
Putting the Pieces Together 127
The Audit 128
The Commitment 129
Developing Strategy 129
Implementing and Executing 130
Refinement 130
Reflection and Application 131

CHAPTER 7: NOT ALL TRAINING IS CREATED EQUAL 133
In This Chapter 133
DEIB Training Failures 134
Training and the Brain 135
Experiential Learning 136
Experiential Learning Best Practices 139
Measuring The Impact of Training 141
Ongoing Comprehensive Training 142
Reflection and Application 149

CHAPTER 8: WHAT YOU FOCUS ON WILL EXPAND 151
In This Chapter 151
Recruiting, Hiring, and Onboarding 153
Compensation 155
Promotions and Advancements 155
General Workplace Policies 156
Metrics 158
Reflection and Application 160

CHAPTER 9: SUPPLIER DIVERSITY 161
In This Chapter 161

BENEFITS & IMPORTANCE OF SUPPLIER DIVERSITY DEVELOPMENT............... 162
ADVANCING SUPPLIER DIVERSITY IN THE SUPPLY CHAIN 163
    Best Practices for Establishing a Supplier
    Diversity Program 164
REFLECTION AND APPLICATION 172

CHAPTER 10: MOVING BEYOND DIVERSITY TO INCLUSION AND BELONGING.. 173
IN THIS CHAPTER 173
DIVERSITY TO INCLUSION.. 174
CULTURE OF INCLUSION.. 176
BELONGING IS THE MISSING PIECE 178
    It Begins with Empathy.. 179
    Stories of Origin 181
REFLECTION AND APPLICATION 182

CHAPTER 11: INCLUSIVE LEADERSHIP 183
IN THIS CHAPTER 183
WHAT IS INCLUSIVE LEADERSHIP 184
WHY INCLUSIVE LEADERSHIP MATTERS 185
    Benefits and Impacts of Inclusive Leadership 186
THE SIGNATURE TRAITS OF INCLUSIVE LEADERS 187
A CHARGE TO ALL LEADERS 202
REFLECTION AND APPLICATION 203

CHAPTER 12: UNPACKING PRIVILEGE: INSIGHTS FOR INCLUSIVE LEADERSHIP 205
IN THIS CHAPTER 205
WHAT IS PRIVILEGE - UNDERSTANDING PRIVILEGE IN EVERYDAY LIFE 206
RECOGNIZING PRIVILEGE IN THE WORKPLACE 206
COMMON MISCONCEPTIONS ABOUT PRIVILEGE 207
DIFFERENT TYPES OF PRIVILEGE 210
    Social and Cultural Privilege.. 211
    Economic, Educational and Network Privilege 212
    Family and Community Privilege 212
    Physical and Health Privilege... 213
    Citizenship, and Environmental Privilege 213
THE IMPORTANCE OF LEADERS UNDERSTANDING PRIVILEGE 214
CHARGE TO LEADERS..216

    Reflection and Application 217

CHAPTER 13: THE TRIAD OF SUCCESS: BUILDING A HIGH-PERFORMANCE CULTURE THROUGH MINDSET, SKILLSET, AND HEARTSET 219

    In This Chapter 219
    The Connection Between DEIB and a High-Performance Culture 220
    Myths About a High Performance Culture 221
        What is a High-Performance Culture? 226
        What is a High-Performance Team? 226
    The Pillars of a High-Performance Culture: Mindset, Skillset, and Heartset 227
    Practical Strategies for Implementing a High-Performance Culture 232
    Reflection and Application 241

CHAPTER 14: IGNITING PASSION: THE POWER OF EMPLOYEE ENGAGEMENT 243

    In This Chapter 243
    Debunking Myths About Employee Engagement 247
    The Impact of Employee Engagement: Fueling Success 249
    Key Metrics for Measuring Employee Engagement 254
    Strategies for Enhancing Employee Engagement 257
    Overlooked Aspects of Employee Engagement 259
    Developing an Action Plan 262
    Fostering Employee Engagement for Organizational Success ... 264
    Reflection and Application 266

CHAPTER 15: THE NEED FOR OUTSIDE PERSPECTIVE 267

    In This Chapter 267
    When You Need A DEIB Expert 268
    Ask Before Hiring 270
    When It's Go Time 271
    Reflection and Application 273

ABOUT THE AUTHOR 275

    iSuccess Business Model 276

PREFACE

Diversity is not a black and white issue. So why do we make it one?

Diversity, Equity, Inclusion, and Belonging (DEIB) is a topic that impacts a company's moral, social, and economic position from the top down with C-Suite executives, board members, directors, managers, employees, stakeholders, suppliers, and their DEIB supporters. It is a widely talked about subject with no lack of emphasis on training or implementing strategies and policies for improving DEIB practices. Yet, so many strategies, training, and commitments to the subject fall short or completely flat. We try to embrace differences by doing what we have always done. Social media, news outlets, even DEIB *experts* and corporate decision makers make it a mostly Black issue.

To continue doing what we have always done only leads to the same results—focusing on one or two groups with little meaningful progress. *Beyond Differences* is different. This is a playbook, a one-stop shop for all things DEIB to give you a well-rounded perspective with actionable strategies with real examples so you can organically implement DEIB easily and with confidence.

This playbook isn't your typical stuffy, dry take on DEIB. All the information, stories, and strategies come from a DEIB expert who has lived on both sides of the fence. First, as someone who was left out of the conversation at an early age but later gained a seat at some of the most impressive board tables in business. Second, the insight and processes have been fine-tuned over decades.

Beyond Differences is a reference guide that works **differently** to entertain while enlightening with a sensible, conversational style that bridges the gaps in current DEIB practices, strategies, and understanding.

INTRODUCTION

Two years ago, I wrote this book and let it gather dust as I observed the landscape of division widening with the repeal of affirmative action, lawsuits, and the growing negative connotations associated with the term "DEIB" (Diversity, Equity, Inclusion and Belonging). Fear and lack of patience was mounting due to misunderstandings about race, privilege, equity, inclusion, and belonging. I hesitated to share this book with the world. At first, it remained buried on my computer, as I was wary of jumping into the public conversation. However, I came to realize that this conversation needed to be had. If not me, then who?

Welcome to *Beyond Differences* —a journey born out of necessity, fueled by conviction, and rooted in the belief that every voice matters. In the rapidly evolving landscape of DEIB, organizations and communities are grappling with unprecedented challenges and opportunities. As our world grows increasingly diverse, the imperative for inclusive workplaces and communities has never been more urgent. Yet, against the backdrop of global uncertainties, heightened racial tensions, and political discord, many of us find ourselves gripped by fear, DEIB fatigue, and apprehension.

But fear not, for within these pages lies a roadmap—a guide to navigate the complexity of our challenges with compassion, patience, and empathy. Here, we'll delve into the interconnectedness of mental health, mindset, and DEIB (Diversity, Equity, and Inclusion and Belonging). This isn't merely a conversation about changing beliefs; it's about creating environments where individuals can authentically be themselves, where values and lived experiences are respected, and where every voice finds its rightful place.

So why should you embark on this journey? Because within these chapters lies the promise of transformation. Together, we'll journey from uncertainty and division to unity and empowerment, where every voice matters and inclusivity thrives. Picture a vibrant, interconnected workspace and community with unique perspectives—where each person strengthens the culture of your organization and enriches the lives of your team members.

The Origin of this Book

I sent my significant other to the store. Among other things, I asked for apples. I knew I should have gone on my own to avoid the inevitable calls and texts that would follow. However, I already had my hands full and delegated! So, as predicted, I got a text:

> *I'm here and grabbing a buggy. Do you want green apples or red?*

I respond:

> *I want both. Get a few Honeycrisps and a couple of Newtown Pippin. Thank you!*

A few minutes later, another text:

> *I found two kinds of Granny Smith apples but not Newtown Pippin. There are organic and regular—also, no Honeycrisp in organic. For red organic, they only have Red Delicious. Have we ever tried Fuji? What about Gala? I didn't realize how many different varieties there are!!*

I laughed. It is a beautiful thing when our eyes are open to the endless possibilities — the variety.

I share my apple story because this is how we have approached diversity in corporate America. We have been so focused on two criteria for decades. For the apples, the focus was color and farming method. In the corporate world, it has been color and gender. We often miss that diversity is much more than color and gender. Like the apples, there is so much more diversity and nuance to consider.

The Depth of Diversity

Our understanding of diversity is often a mile wide and an inch deep. In other words, we only scratch the surface. For so long, companies have committed to being diverse and inclusive. They give their best effort. Yet, conversations go something like this — We need more women leaders and more people of color to hold managerial positions. What we focus on expands. So, companies will strive to make some changes and then proudly report to the media their numbers of women employees or Black managers. There is a clear conversation.

To be fair, the focus on women and Black people comes from squeaky wheels and our history in the US. Women spoke out for the right to vote. Black people and supporters spoke out against slavery. Then we had the civil rights movement and feminist movements. There is a long history and focus on equity for these two groups.

While we have focused on strategies to improve equity and inclusion for these two groups, we seem to forget that there are so many other groups when we talk about diversity. For some, their voice isn't as loud and doesn't get the media attention it deserves. I am talking about the neurodivergent, the LGBTQ+[1] community or the lesser talked about groups from different socioeconomic backgrounds, single mothers, older workers, veterans, members of the disability community, and those with nontraditional educational backgrounds. Diversity is more than race and gender — it is about the diversity of thought, opinions, ideas and varied views. It's also about cognitive diversity, the variety of perspectives, problem-solving styles, and thinking patterns among individuals within a group or organization.

The workforce is like the apple section at the grocery store. Every apple might be part of a particular group, but each one is a different shape, size, and character. Our diversity is rich, and there is so much more depth than we recognize on the surface. Every human has a personal history, a story, and a background full of experiences, and it is this uniqueness that brings different perspectives, new ideas, and alternative solutions to problems.

But You Ask, What's in It for Me?

Let's be honest, trying to sell to your predominantly white board of directors, C-Suite executives, or shareholders that you need to

---

[1] NOTE that the LGBTQ acronym is fluid and changes depending on whom you talk to. Therefore, LGBTQ+ is used.

INTRODUCTION

release the purse strings on a DEIB budget just because it's the right thing to do isn't going to fly many times. They want to know how or if it will positively impact the company — how it will affect your bottom line. They're not interested in carve-outs or set-asides that take money out of the pocket of friends. You know, the college frat buddies, neighbors, etc.

Don't get me wrong; there are still some good-hearted leaders that want to do what's right because it's right, but then there are the ones that will go along kicking and screaming because DEIB is the new wave of the organization. Which one are they? Which are you? No need to raise your hand; we can't see you.

If the bottom line matters most, we now have plenty of data to support the need for DEIB strategies and going all in. For those companies who have put all the chips in on diversity, they are admittedly reaping the benefits. Perhaps the most eye-catching for executives and shareholders is the bottom line. McKinsey released their Diversity Wins report.[2] In it, they reported that,

> "Of more than 1,000 companies in 15 countries found that organizations in the top quartile of gender diversity were more likely to **outperform on profitability**—25% more likely for gender diverse executive teams and 28% more likely for gender-diverse boards. Organizations in the top quartile for ethnic/cultural diversity among executives were 36% more likely to achieve above-average profitability. At the other end of the spectrum, companies in the bottom quartile for both gender and ethnic/

---

[2] https://www.mckinsey.com/featured-insights/diversity-and-inclusion/diversity-wins-how-inclusion-matters#

cultural diversity were 27% *less* likely to experience profitability above the industry average."[3]

Many other studies show that diversity improves innovation and workforce performance and builds brand loyalty. So, while having diversity is the right thing to do, it is also a sound business decision.

iSuccess wants your business to be more profitable and have an enhanced social conscious. So, we offer you *Beyond Differences*, the DEIB Playbook. It is a comprehensive Diversity, Equity, Inclusion and Belonging (DEIB) resource tool that challenges the stale and ineffective practices we are used to. You can work through the book from beginning to end or flip through the chapters out of sequence for quick guidance. The information is easily digestible, aiming to enhance your understanding in a lighthearted yet sensible way.

What this book is not — This is not your old boring conversation about diversity. We need a new way of thinking to bridge the willing and unwilling — the aware and unaware — those that are trying and those that are not. It is not about picking sides and doing something to meet a quota. It is about gaining an understanding and a sense of belonging for an organically diverse space for everyone. After all, as humans, we seek acceptance, and we all want to be a part of a community.

Beyond Differences offers strategies you can easily embed in your organization with examples of real-life applications. C-Suite leaders will gain a better understanding of DEIB. They will gain insights and talking points to use with internal and external

---

[3] https://www.catalyst.org/research/why-diversity-and-inclusion-matter-financial-performance/#:~:text=The%20study%20found%20higher%20levels,who%20do%20not%20(13%25)

stakeholders and help understand how to lead a team with differences. Further, because most DEIB and Supplier Diversity Departments are small and underfunded, Beyond Differences is an excellent start to help Directors and Executive VPs develop an affordable DEIB strategy that you can roll out corporate-wide with the assistance of iSuccess Consulting.

You do not need to be a decision maker or rocket scientist to understand, live, and work by what the Playbook offers. On the contrary, the Playbook can also be adopted by people leaders and employees. It will help people leaders gain a clearer understanding of DEIB and how to lead their team with empathy, cultural intelligence, and knowledge of their own unconscious bias and how to deal with it. For employees, it will help them understand how to relate to others with differences and become better allies and collaborators.

Finally, the Playbook is for future practitioners of DEIB, lovers of DEIB, including historians, motivational speakers, influencers, and supporters of DEIB work. It will give those who want to enter the field or speak on the topic a comprehensive perspective of DEIB. The Playbook is all things diversity with a bit of spice.

Before You Begin

As you read through the pages of this book, don't get overwhelmed by thinking about **"HOW"** you will wrap your head around DEIB. Focus more on the "WHY" it's important to support DEIB for your organization, and "WHO" can help you on this journey. By the end of our time together, you'll likely discover that I'm your **"WHO."** Our team takes a very non-threatening and engaging approach to building bridges to

INTRODUCTION

develop diverse, equitable, inclusive, and belonging spaces where everybody thrives.

Let your DEIB Journey Begin.

> **Diversity is having a seat at the table, Inclusion is having a voice, and belonging is having that voice be heard.**
>
> — LIZ FOSSLIEN

CHAPTER 1

EVOLUTION OF DIVERSITY

> *An individual has not started living until he can rise above the narrow confines of his individualistic concerns to the broader concerns of all humanity.*
> ~ Martin Luther King, Jr

In This Chapter:

- History's impact on DEIB
- Timeline of DEIB in the Workplace
- Redefining Diversity
- Four Types of Diversity
- Reflection and Application

Any conversation about diversity, equity, inclusion and Belonging (DEIB) should begin with an understanding of history. And not just the vanilla version of history taught in our public schools. Nor should it be a summary of the thirty-second snippets we see on social media or in the news. While we live in a society of instant gratification and have immediate access to information, we need to step back and take an unbiased look at the history of DEIB.

A Historian's Perspective

JUST BECAUSE YOU ARE RIGHT, DOES NOT MEAN, I AM WRONG. YOU JUST HAVEN'T SEEN LIFE FROM MY SIDE.

If we take a minute and look at DEIB through the lens of the historian, we can gain a better perspective and understanding that will lead to more enriched conversations that are more inclusive. A more inclusive dialogue can bring more willing participation from all sides.

With everything, we all have a bias. It is impossible to avoid having a personal slant to everything we see, hear, interpret or do. However, historians are a little different — they are a different breed, so to speak. This is not to say they are absent of bias. On the contrary, they are human, and it is unavoidable. However, they are highly aware of bias. Whether academically or professionally trained, historians are educated on bias. They do not try to hide, cover-up, or spin bias. As a matter of fact, they push it to the forefront. Historians argue with each other — respectfully. It is a process of keeping their bias in check.

Historians are introduced to and often agree to adhere to the Statement on Standards and Professional Conduct through the American Historical Association. At its core, the statement speaks to historians practicing with integrity and understanding that they have a limited view,

> *"But the very nature of our discipline means that historians also understand that all knowledge is situated in time and place, that all interpretations express a point of view, and that no mortal mind can ever aspire to omniscience. Because the record of the past is so fragmentary, absolute historical knowledge is denied us."*.[4]

Because historians recognize bias, they work to see and interpret history through the eyes of the ones who lived it. They consider multiple competing or conflicting perspectives.

When teaching history, the Statement of Standards says,

> *"Good teaching entails accuracy and rigor in communicating factual information and strives always to place such*

---

[4] https://www.historians.org/jobs-and-professional-development/statements-standards-and-guidelines-of-the-discipline/statement-on-standards-of-professional-conduct

information in context to convey its larger significance. Integrity in teaching means presenting competing interpretations with fairness and intellectual honesty."

The point here is that there is a connection between history and DEIB practices. Each often brings multiple conflicting and competing perspectives. So, when we talk about DEIB, just as when we discuss the history of things, it is usually best to turn to the practices of the historians, understanding there is bias and seeking information from many different perspectives. This can lead to fruitful discussions rather than arguments, bridging the current gaps in DEIB progress.

History's Impact on DEI

I know, nobody needs a history lesson. We seem to get enough of that by turning to social media or the news. So, this will be brief. When we start a conversation about history's impact on DEI, we have to go back centuries and consider the broad scope of the written word from ancient times to the present. Throughout history, we have found undisputed artifacts with writing. Human nature and curiosity have led civilizations to designate interpreters and translators to make sense of symbols, hieroglyphs, and written words for hundreds of years. More often than not, these interpreters and translators were educated men. And often, the text was misinterpreted.

Now, please stick with me. We are not heading into a black and white argument. This isn't the white male is to blame attack. This is a journey of perspective.

In almost every culture, men were explorers, crusaders, traders, colonizers, conquerors, or warriors. By default, they came in contact with and had to learn to communicate and interpret different languages, cultures, and customs. For the most part, women stayed home.

Through the centuries, predominantly European men began the colonization of countries around the world. They would explore and research new land, cultures, and customs, then write about their encounters through the lens of a biased perspective. Decades passed with their interpretations and findings settling as undisputed history.

Look at our history books and interpretations of these explorations and discoveries. We have a plethora of written records from many sources — all with similar accounts. Explorers would pen about savages, heathens, and untamed children. Other explorers concur. Meanwhile, those they encountered often had well-formed societies, beliefs, and customs that were often more exacting than those who discredited them.

Now, this is a very simplistic summary of history only to highlight the point that historical interpretations and impressions that have been handed down for centuries were initially founded on the predominantly educated male perspective. It wasn't until fairly recently that we began to see that many translations and views were biased, and records are now being re-examined.

Historical Diversity

Have you ever read the book *Lies My Teacher Told Me: Everything Your American History Book Got Wrong*? Written in 1995, the author, James W. Loewen, criticizes American History textbooks for their biased Eurocentric and mythologized views of history. He also offers alternative perspectives that he felt should be taught. This book, Beyond Differences, is the *Lies My Teacher Told Me* DEI equivalent.

I compare the two (history and DEI) because they are intertwined. After all, it wasn't until fairly recent decades that we began to hear and consider other historical perspectives and interpretations, leading to discussions of diversity. All our laws, business practices, and values have been derived from an engrained perspective — passed down for centuries. Whether we believe it or not, society is founded on very distinct ideals.

One of the most noted, written discussions about historical interpretations is that of the late Peter Novick of the University of Chicago. He wrote *That Noble Dream: The "Objectivity Question" and the American Historical Profession* (1988). He scoured historical archives and papers documenting how accepted ideas, interpretations, and methodologies arose, resulting in a historical consensus. He uncovered alternative perspectives of history, methodologies, and approaches and shared how the 1950s and 60s brought with them an enlightening or new analysis of social and women's history in particular.[5]

Novick's research on expanding diversity in historical analysis paved the way for history to grow beyond the one-dimensional. He recognized the historical writings and teachings of many groups with diverse perspectives. Interestingly these differing perspectives didn't really rise to the foreground until the civil and women's rights movements.

As we well know, change is complex and often not positively received. Even in our day-to-day routine, change isn't always embraced. Think about those minor irritations that force you to make a change. You go to the coffee shop, and they are out of your favorite coffee, or your car broke down, so you have to ride the bus or take an Uber—a minor change that comes with minor inconveniences. Now consider systemic change on a large scale.

Changing perspective, policies, and practices as it relates to history, is not so simple — it is diverse. History is complex, questioned, and debated as it should be. And history, with all the complexity, is interwoven with DEI efforts. History offers insight into how we got to where we are.

So, why the long-winding explanation of history in the context of DEI?

Because — our history, cultural norms, and communities were all built on systemic racism and **unconscious bias**. We must understand the root cause and our contributions to racist behaviors, policies, and practices. Once we understand that bias exists and has played a role in our countries, cultures, and personal histories, we can then work to fix it.

---

[5] https://www.historians.org/publications-and-directories/perspectives-on-history/may-2016/diversity-among-historical-practitioners-in-research-and-in-teaching

Unconscious Bias – *The social stereotypes we have about certain people or groups of people that we are unaware of.*

The Systemic Racism Conversation

When looking at the impact of history on DEI efforts, we have to determine how far back we want to travel and what we want to focus on. The subject is so vast that we could start back with colonization and human rights. We could jump forward to focus on American history and the formation of the Constitution, later Amendments, and the Bill of Rights. It all plays a significant role in bringing us where we are today.

However, the promise to refrain from old, traditional, vapid commentary still holds true. Without preaching and polarized political propaganda, let's look at the impact from a different perspective starting with the civil rights era and social capital.

I will not rehash the conversations about systemic racism. I hope we can all agree that before the civil rights era, our country had laws, policies, and practices that significantly impacted women, people of color, aging adults, and the disabled. Those laws, policies, and practices were based on historical biases and social norms of the times. They would not have existed if they were not considered socially or morally acceptable at the time.

That is where social capital comes into play. In the past, underrepresented groups didn't have the social capital or the backing to push awareness or policies. It wasn't until the civil rights movement that systemic racism was questioned with enough support to move the country forward.

Social Capital Contributions

Capital is generally defined as an asset — something that we can use, combine, exchange, or invest for benefits (security, wealth, enrichment, etc.). Therefore, social capital is the benefits derived from being social.[6] They are those social assets — usually the time, energy, assistance, influence, etc. we will give or hope to receive through connections and relationships. We use, build, leverage, or accumulate social capital to gain benefit in some way. As it relates to DEI, social capital is and has been the time, energy, assistance, influence, relationships, and connections used to build DEI awareness and later policies that benefit under-represented groups.

---

[6] https://www.socialcapitalresearch.com/what-is-social-capital/

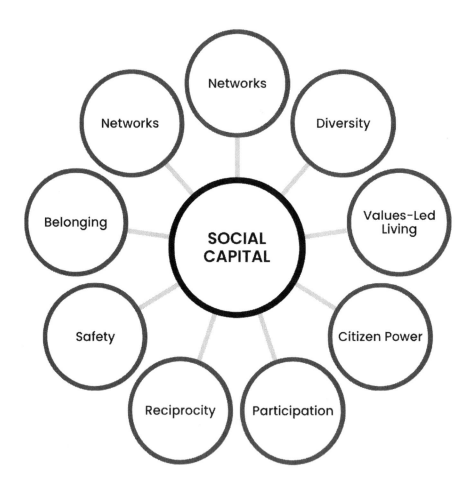

There are three types of social capital:

- **Bonding** – Bonding would be the strongest type of social capital consisting of close relationships between two or more people with shared characteristics who developed a bond through close social ties. Think of the co-worker who becomes a close friend or the friendship that developed from participating in a hobby. It could also be a neighbor or family member. When closely bonded, we will most often invest social capital (our time, energy, and assistance).

- **Bridging** – Bridging is social capital between friends of friends or acquaintances. Unlike bonding, where there are similarities in characteristics, bridging involves an intermediary — the bridge to make a social connection. Bridging is about bringing two are more people together who may not otherwise make association but are in the same social circles horizontally. Think of when you ask a close friend for a recommendation. They bridge you with the doctor, plumber, landscaper, or stylist.

- **Linking** - is similar to bridging in that it will bridge or link individuals. The very significant difference is that linking is vertical. Bridging brings people together in a horizontal direction with similar socioeconomic status or interests. Whereas linking crosses vertically to connect individuals between the differing levels of the societal power hierarchy.[7]

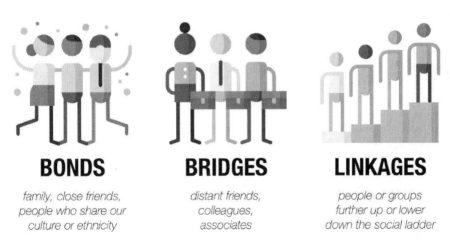

BONDS
family, close friends, people who share our culture or ethnicity

BRIDGES
distant friends, colleagues, associates

LINKAGES
people or groups further up or lower down the social ladder

Throughout history, we have experienced social capital contributions to DEI. Some may argue it started with President

---

[7] https://www.socialcapitalresearch.com/what-is-linking-social-capital/

Lincoln. Yet, the most notable acceleration in social capital contributions would be from the time leading up to the civil rights movement to the present. The acceleration is undoubtedly linked to awareness, a massive effort to leverage all three types of social capital (from the top down and grassroots up), and the explosion of information through mass media — at the time, television.

Countless people used or offered social capital contributions. Whether you like him or not, President Truman, even with his DEI faults, desegregated the military and started the President's Committee on Civil Rights. Were you ever taught about Walter Reuther, Barbara Henry, or Morris Dees? Each risked their social and professional standing and gave social capital to the DEI cause in courageous ways. No doubt there were thousands more that will always remain nameless.

The point is that much of this social capital was leveraged when we also had a jump on the technology horizon. While television had been accessible in the late 1940s, it didn't find its way into the average home until 1951. In the mid-1940s, there were less than 10,000 televisions in use. By the mid-1950s, half of all US homes had one.[8] The media captured the reality of the struggles in real time and allowed Americans to witness some of the brutalities taking place.

Bearing witness to the conflict, the riots, and the marches gave rise to an awareness — an awakening. Those with social connections and high social capital felt obligated to use their standing and capital to drive changes. The amount of bonding, bridging, and linking was like no other time in our history.

When you think about it, the acceleration of DEI efforts through the 1960s was a catapult to where we are. Look at the timeline for perspective.

---

[8] https://stephens.hosting.nyu.edu/History%20of%20Television%20page.html#:~:text=The%20number%20of%20television%20sets,all%20U.S.%20homes%20had%20one.

A Timeline of DEI Relating to Corporate Initiatives

- **1948** – President Truman desegregates the Military
- **1961** – President Kennedy signs the Affirmative Action Executive Order
- **1964** – The Civil Rights Act is made law, and the Equal Employment Opportunity Commission is established.
- **1972** - EEOC wins Supreme Court Case earning the right to sue companies for discrimination. Companies begin affirmative action training.
- **1974** - Black employees at Xerox form independent caucus groups.
- **1987** - The Hudson Institute releases the Workforce 2000 study predicting the workforce will be predominantly female, older, and more racially and multiculturally diverse.
- **1990** - Americans with Disabilities Act was signed into law.
- **1993** - The Family and Medical Leave Act becomes law.
- **2000** - The position of Chief Diversity Officer rises.
- **2009** - Ursula Vums becomes the first Black female CEO of a Fortune 500 company.
- **2009** - The Lilly Ledbetter Act gives protections against pay discrimination.
- **2013** - Growing research documents the high cost of discrimination and bias.
- **2013** - The rise of Black Lives Matter

- **2014** - Google is the first tech company to release a diversity report.

- **2016** - A wave of CEOs speak out against North Carolina's anti-LGBTQ law.

- **2017** - Journalists start a global movement exposing sexual abuse and assault, resulting in 200 executives losing their jobs.

- **2018** - 145 Fortune 500 companies report at least 40% diversity on their boards.

- **2022 to Present** - The number of Fortune 500 companies with diverse CEOs returns to a record high. CEOs recognize that DEIB is not a one-off box to check. DEIB now targets Diversity, Equity, Inclusion and Belonging.

"THE CEO SAYS WE NEED TO FOCUS ON DIVERSITY. HIRE PEOPLE THAT LOOK DIFFERENT, BUT THINK JUST LIKE ME."

Are we done? Can we sit back now? Unfortunately, the answer is no. I know — I hear the moans and groans, the mumbling and grumbling in the back — but hear me out.

You may think that HR has it under control. We no longer have major DEIB issues. Or, we have taken so much sensitivity training; what else is there? I would offer that the DEIB conversation, in many ways, has become more divisive and staler, and it seems that despite all the forward progress, the conversation isn't over. The conversation has taken a turn but not in a meaningful forward direction. As a matter of fact, the conversation, in many ways, has waned even with all the media attention it still receives. Have you heard remarks like *why are we still doing this sensitivity training? It doesn't make a difference.*

Diversity and the conversation still matter. At issue is how we are approaching it. We are using old methods and bias in our approach. We need a refresh — a redo. The spectrum of diversity has grown, and we have learned so much more. With new information, we need to adapt to higher levels of interaction and incorporation.

So many think that diversity is a women's or black and white issue. But have you considered what is going on in the socioeconomic sphere? We have a rising population that lives with food scarcity or is homeless. The poor are not only discriminated against, but we continue to use antiquated formulas for addressing housing, employment, health, and education for this sector of society. We also continue to make assumptions about socioeconomic status among the BIPOC population.

We need a fresh and broader perspective — more immersive DEIB strategies.

Think of it like the internet. Are you old enough to remember that first dial-up internet connection and the World Wide Web? You used the phone's landline to connect. You hear the beeps and boops and wah-lah! You are connected to AOL. For the younger crowd, AOL was Flintstone's version of today's Google. Of course, if you don't know AOL, you probably don't know the Flintstones. Maybe the picture will help.

I digress. When connected to AOL, you could check and send email messages and go to websites to read what was there. It was a one-dimensional source of obtaining information. It was an online library and a faster version of snail mail. Desegregation of the military, the Civil Rights Act, and other legislation were DEIB 1.0.

Eventually, we evolved to Web 2.0. That is what we have now. You can directly interact in real-time. We have Facetime, Skype, Zoom, and chatbots. We can create, buy, sell and interact with almost everything we touch. We get instant response and gratification. Yet, this is two-dimensional. This is where we are now. There is a two-way interaction with DEIB. We have in-person training, a feedback loop within HR departments, etc.

Most recently is Web 3.0. This is your virtual reality where you can now interact with holograms and visit places in three dimensions. Now, instead of seeing a picture of the inside of a building, you can virtually stand in the building. You can look up or down, side to side, and move from one place to another.

We need to bring forward the Web 3.0 version of DEIB. We need to upgrade the conversation, innovate, and have strategies that aren't focused on old and outdated information and conversations.

There is still a need and strong business case for this evolution.

Redefining Diversity

If we continue to do what we have always done, we will keep getting the same results. Think about how you define diversity. Diversity means different things to different people. Do you define it based on the legislation that has been enacted? Do you formulate your definition based on the news or social media? Does your inner circle or culture come into play when you define diversity?

For so many, there is a belief that diversity is just a Black issue. Some may stretch and even include it as a women's issue. We are missing so much more of the conversation. Diversity has been made a black or gender issue that we rarely hear a discussion about ageism (unless you are over fifty) or first-generation college graduates.

Because everyone has different concepts of diversity, it seems appropriate to start with clear definitions of what diversity is and isn't. Yes, DEIB includes diversity, equity, and inclusion. But there is also belonging, accessibility, anti-racism, justice, and BIPOC (Black Indigenous People of Color). For our purposes, these are the definitions for each:

- **Diversity** - Is variety and variation in characteristics. It is the condition of being composed of different elements. Diversity is the mix of components or characteristics like race, gender, religion, sexual orientation, age, abilities, disabilities, exceptionalities, culture, ideas, socioeconomic status, geographic background, political leanings, experiences, beliefs, and worldview. Diversity also includes tolerance, immersion, and coexistence of all the above. It is not enough to introduce or have all the different elements to say you are diverse. We often miss the link between tolerance, immersion, and coexistence.

- **Equity** - In the strictest sense, equity is the "state, quality or ideal of being just, impartial and fair." We often confuse equity with equality. But they are far from the same. Equity is the process of trying to understand and give people what they need to be happy, healthy, or successful. On the other hand, equality aims to give everyone the same thing to achieve health, happiness, or success. What we need is never the exact same. We don't NEED equality in offerings or opportunities; we need equity. We need equal ACCESS to offerings and opportunities. For example, everyone has equal access to maternity leave (in broad, simple terms). Yet, someone who never plans to have children may need time to care for an aging parent, not maternity leave. See the difference?

- **Inclusion** - To be invited to participate or given equal access is only part of the definition of inclusion. Inclusion also means that individuals are treated fairly and respectfully. They have equal access AND opportunity to CONTRIBUTE to the group. It is not enough to allow access and then discount or ignore contributions.

- **Belonging** - A sense of belonging is essential when talking about DEIB. Belonging is that sense of feeling happy, content, and comfortable in a group. Belonging goes beyond inclusion, equality, and equity. When your people have a sense of belonging, you know your DEIB efforts are working!

- **Accessibility** – Accessibility ensures that everyone, regardless of background or ability, can access opportunities, resources, and services. It involves creating inclusive workplaces, removing barriers in communities, and ensuring that customer services are usable by all. This includes physical and digital accessibility, accommodations for disabilities, and practices that support diverse needs. Accessibility is about fostering environments where everyone can fully participate and thrive.

- **Anti-Racism** - To say you are against racism is not anti-racism. Anti-racism is the active process of identifying, opposing, and challenging racism to change policies, practices, beliefs, and behaviors that continue to propagate racism. To say one isn't racist thinking they can avoid participation falls short of what anti-racism is. Anti-racism is about action, not words. If we don't work to dismantle racism actively, we continue to live with our unconscious bias.

- **Justice** - Justice is about leveling the playing field and creating a world where everyone is treated with fairness, equity and accountability. This involves addressing discrimination, bias, and systemic inequities to promote transparency, integrity, and ethical conduct. It encompasses providing equitable access to opportunities, resources, and services, fostering inclusive environments where all individuals are treated with dignity and respect.

- **BIPOC** - Pronounced "bye-pock," stands for Black, Indigenous, and People of Color and is considered person-first language. The acronym helps us move away from terms like 'marginalized' and 'minority.' While these terms are technically or factually correct, they lack sensitivity and carry a connotation of inferiority. The first use of BIPOC happened in the 2010s and didn't become more widespread until early 2020 on social media. This could be considered one of those blimps heading into DEIB 3.0. Progress but not perfection!

With a few terms out of the way, let's move on. Did you know there are four different types of diversity? Do you know what they are? Have you ever heard of them? More than likely, you have, but never placed them in context.

Four Types of Diversity

When we think of diversity, we usually limit our perception to workplace diversity. After all, we have been told this is where it really matters. Remember the conversation on our mile-wide and inch-deep understanding of diversity. This is where we find the depth. The types of diversity are like dimensions of diversity. Like an onion — diversity has layers! Should I quote Donkey from the Shrek movie on that?

The four types or dimensions of diversity are internal, external, organizational, and worldview. Let's break them down and eat the elephant one bite at a time!

- **Internal Diversity** - is what makes each of us unique individuals. This includes all the characteristics that make up who we are, such as our gender, age, ethnicity, cultural background, physical abilities and appearance, sexual orientation, personality, education, and life experiences. We all have different combinations of these characteristics, which contribute to our overall individuality.

- **External Diversity** - is everything that exists outside of us as individuals. It encompasses the social environment in which we live and work, including factors such as family status, socioeconomic class, religion, and political beliefs. It also includes the organizations we belong to, our communities, and the larger society in which we exist. All of these external factors can influence our individual behavior and attitudes.

- **Organizational Diversity** - encompasses how organizations are structured and operate. This includes things like company size, industry type, geographical location, and company culture. Each organization has its unique combination of these characteristics, which can impact how employees interact and do business.

- **Worldview Diversity** - refers to the different ways people see and understand the world around them. This can be influenced by cultural values, religious beliefs, economic status, and life experiences. People with different worldviews can have very different perspectives on issues and problems.

With so many variables, it is easy to see why out-of-the-box DEIB strategies might fail, right?

> **REFLECTION AND APPLICATION**
>
> - With a better understanding of bias, the old versus new definitions of diversity, history, and the different types of diversity, what is the biggest takeaway?
> - Did anything surprise you?
> - Is there anything in your current DEIB practices or policies that you feel could be updated with this information?

CHAPTER 2

WHY DIVERSITY MATTERS

> *"When we're talking about diversity, it's not a box to check. It is a reality that should be deeply felt and held and valued by all of us."*
>
> – Ava Duvernay, American Filmmaker

In This Chapter

- The Business Case of DEIB
- Results of Properly Implementing DEIB
- Why Most DEIB Initiatives Fail
- Barriers to DEIB
- Overcoming Barriers
- DEIB Best Practices
- Reflection and Application

For decades studies have shown a business case for having strong DEIB strategies and policies. The arguments for better profits and returns have undoubtedly helped push diversity efforts. However, there is more to the conversation than increased profits. As a matter of fact, many are not impressed with DEIB efforts when they only focus on the bottom line. Further, some companies have found that specific DEIB efforts can increase costs or liabilities or create a toxic culture of tokenism. The conversation has taken a turn, and the business case for DEIB may not be what you think any longer.

Business Case for DEIB

Consensus used to say that if you focus on hiring BIPOC, women, those with disabilities, and members of the LGBTQ+[9] community, you not only fill your moral and legal obligations, but you will automatically see profits increase. What we are now finding out is that isn't always the case.

Diversity doesn't automatically ensure higher profitability. Nor does screaming your commitment to diversity from the rooftops attract diverse talent. As a matter of fact, new research shows that the business case for diversity can and is backfiring with underrepresented groups.[10] Organizations that make the financial business case for diversity undermine the anticipated sense of belonging of the underrepresented individuals. Further, these underrepresented individuals are less attracted to the organization. Diverse professionals already within the organization who are or feel tokenized will jump ship. Finally, when diverse

---

[9] NOTE that the LGBTQ acronym is fluid and changes depending on whom you talk to. Therefore, LGBTQ+ is used.
[10] https://pubmed.ncbi.nlm.nih.gov/35679195/

professionals are perceived as less qualified, it can impact the organizational culture as well as investor interest:

> *"Investors may take note of poor DEI policies and may penalize firms by ascribing lower valuations. For example, research examining diversity that is mandated by regulators shows that when boards are forced to diversify by adding less qualified directors, it results in lower firm value. In the PE [private equity]* "*industry specifically, there is evidence that investors see through attempts by general partners to "window dress" return performance, so it may not be unreasonable to expect the same is true for evaluations of DEI success."*[11]

---

[11] https://kenaninstitute.unc.edu/kenan-insight/a-different-business-case-for-diversity/#:~:text=In%20response%2C%20businesses%20have%20renewed,to%20achieve%20their%20diversity%20goals.

Let me say it louder for those in the back —

You cannot implement a DEIB strategy that doesn't have a holistic business case for it or buy-in for all the stakeholders. Half-hearted attempts just don't cut it anymore. Kenan Institute says a DEI business case focused only on financial performance is a poor practice. This is not to say that financial performance doesn't matter, and there is no longer a case showing a positive correlation. It just shouldn't be the only point you hang your hat on.

The more holistic approach comes from a moral position. There is a case to be made that you will have economic benefits by doing the right thing. Part of the economic impact comes from threats. The Kenan Institute argues that *"companies not adopting effective DEI policies face threats on a variety of fronts, ranging from attracting talent to regulatory intervention to pressure from outside investors."*

So, the best justification for diversity is no justification. The study referenced above was conducted by Aneeta Rattan, a professor at London Business School, and she said that when the business case for diversity was read by underrepresented individuals it,

> *"Made members of these underrepresented groups feel like they would be seen as interchangeable. It's kind of like being known as the Black engineer or the woman professor. These people were reporting feeling depersonalized by the business case."*

Based on her research, she argues that we don't make business cases for company values or our mission, so why do we feel we need to justify diversity.[12]

---

[12] https://www.forbes.com/sites/kimelsesser/2022/06/20/the-business-case-for-diversity-is-backfiring/?sh=5ddad39e351d

Now, of course, in reality, we often need a business case to get funding approval for DEIB initiatives or policies. For this, we must form the conversation around proven results when properly implementing DEIB. It isn't just about profits. It is the overall value of the program we implement. The ROI for DEIB isn't always in dollars and cents, but sadly, we often have to justify the dollars and cents. I get it — so let's talk about it!

Results of Properly Implementing DEIB

When promptly implementing a DEIB strategy or framework with immediate and tangible results, you build a solid foundation for DEIB success. But what is success? What does DEIB success look like to you? Is it different than what it looks like to your team? What results can or should you expect from the proper execution of strategy?

We don't have to look too far for guidance. McKinsey & Company has been tracking results of diversity for years. In 2015, they reported that companies in the top twenty-five percent for racial and ethnic diversity were "35% more likely to have financial returns above their respective national industry medians."[13] Gender diversity proved to raise the odds of higher financial returns by fifteen percent. This same report argued there "for every 10 percent increase in racial and ethnic diversity of the senior-executive team, earnings before interest and taxes (EBIT) rise 0.8 percent."

McKinsey & Company updated their report in 2018, showing that there is still a direct relationship between DEI and financial

---

[13] https://www.mckinsey.com/business-functions/people-and-organizational-performance/our-insights/why-diversity-matters

performance. Not only that but there is a clear cost to a lack of DEI within an organization. Financial performance for the top quarter of companies with ethnic and racial diversity ranked very similarly, with a 33% increase in profitability. However, there was a significant change in gender diversity. The percentage for the top quarter moved from 15% to 21% more likely to have above-average EBIT. For the companies with the most ethnically and culturally diverse boards, that number goes to 43%.[14]

The numbers don't lie. So, do you follow the numbers or look the other way?

[14] https://www.mckinsey.com/~/media/mckinsey/business%20functions/people%20and%20organizational%20performance/our%20insights/delivering%20through%20diversity/delivering-through-diversity_full-report.pdf

Yes, your organization could be more profitable with properly implemented DEIB strategies and frameworks. The keywords are PROPERTY IMPLEMENTED—execution matters. Remember the conversation about poor execution and the tokenization of underrepresented individuals? So, when talking about profiting from DEIB, I advise caution because profits are not promised with DEIB if done incorrectly.

However, there are many other benefits to DEIB. Let me count the ways!

DEIB is a Competitive Edge

If you want to beat your competition, listen up! DEIB is your ticket to improved business outcomes like:

- **Innovation** – A BCG (Boston Consulting Group) study from 2017 reports that when you have teams with diverse backgrounds and experiences, they tend to look at problems differently. This nonlinear thinking drives teams to recognize new market potential, opportunities, and solutions. Problem-solving responsive increases and allows companies to adapt more quickly to keep pace with the rapidly changing business environment.[15]

- **Recruiting and Retaining Top Talent** – When we talk DEI, we get hyper-focused on gender, ethnicity, race, and even LGBTQ+. However, the talent pool is so much bigger! Have you opened the doors to neurodiversity? Think STEM (Science Technology Engineering Math).

---

[15] https://www.bcg.com/en-us/publications/2018/how-diverse-leadership-teams-boost-innovation

You know, all the really smart kids who didn't get picked for the team in gym class. In 2020, SRG Talent reported on GCHQ, which employed over 100 dyslexic and dyspraxic individuals as 'neurodiverse spies' to "harness their ability to decipher facts from patterns, their increased 3D spatial-perception, and their creativity."[16] Broadening your perspective on diversity will help you get through the talent drought we are experiencing.

- **Employee Satisfaction**- In 2021, Zippia reported its workforce diversity findings. Their survey showed that "American employees who think their employer is 'not doing enough' to prioritize diversity have a Workforce Happiness Index score of 63, almost 10 points under the average score of 72."[17] Zippia also reported that performance rates were 35% higher, with diversity higher than the national demographic average.

- **Improved Customer Orientation** – The customer base is increasingly diverse, and those with a diverse organization will connect better with the customer perspective and decision-making. The McKinsey Diversity Matters study reports that women make the majority of purchasing decisions and are expected to own over half of all personal wealth. The buying power of the LGBTQ+ and Black communities is growing as well.

- **Better Decision Making** – Diversity requires teams to expect dissent and to be questioned about their method-

---

[16] https://www.srgtalent.com/blog/diversity-with-a-recruitment-partner
[17] https://www.zippia.com/advice/diversity-in-the-workplace-statistics/#:~:text=Diverse%20companies%20have%20more%20satisfied,the%20average%20score%20of%2072.

ology. Diversity forces teams to think, rethink and then provide support for their solutions. The different perspectives enable team members and the organization to explore a broader range of options to solve problems and do so with more confidence.[18]

- **Diverse Customer Base** - Customers are increasingly more savvy thanks to technology and social media. They have choices and, over the years, have worked to align their purchases with companies with the same beliefs. In 2021, McKinsey reported that two-thirds of Americans said their values shape their purchasing decisions. Further, "the inclusive consumer has the power to influence all demographics."[19]

- **Improved Company Reputation** – Common sense says that when you are doing the right thing because it is the right thing to do, you will be seen more positively. Don't believe it? There is a study for that! One study proved that when companies highlight their diversity, there is the expectation that the company will have "a broadminded and tolerate climate."[20]

So, you say — *yeah, I get it!* Maybe you think — **This isn't anything new.**

You know it's important. You've tried but haven't seen movement. You still have a largely homogeneous organization and

---

[18] https://www.mckinsey.com/~/media/mckinsey/business%20functions/people%20and%20organizational%20performance/our%20insights/why%20diversity%20matters/diversity%20matters.pdf

[19] https://www.mckinsey.com/industries/retail/our-insights/the-rise-of-the-inclusive-consumer

[20] https://journals.sagepub.com/doi/pdf/10.1177/0361684318800264

can't seem to figure out why your DEIB initiatives fail. You feel like you have continued to beat your head against the wall.

Most likely, it isn't just one thing.

Why Most DEIB Initiatives Fail

DEIB isn't as easy as it seems. You can't have a board meeting, commit to increasing your diversity, and then send out a memo to make it so. Further, employees (try as they may) can't shift the culture from a grassroots level if those in the ivory tower are disconnected. DEIB requires a synergy from top to bottom and back up. Most initiatives will fail due to three things — a lack of transparency and trust, lack of support, and lack of action or poorly executed activities. Let's break them down, so you see what I mean.

Lack of Transparency and Trust

A successful DEIB program needs ownership from the top. C-Suite, executives, board members, and leaders often seem too busy to immerse themselves in the process. If you are unwilling to sit with your employees and go through training and education with them or LEAD it, you fail to align what you say with what you do. You have to engage in building trust for the process and in having your DEIB efforts taken seriously.

Further, leadership is often focused on diversity numbers and not giving attention to cultural transformation. How often have you heard (or said) you wanted to increase your woman leadership to X% by a given date? Maybe you have sent a memo during or after an earnings call that you have met your woman leadership goal. You fail to mention how this increase connects to the culture or impacts the organizational culture. Do you thank these women for the insight? Do you focus on women only and not consider the neurodivergent, veterans, or first-generation Black college graduates?

What can be even worse is if you are or have initiated a DEIB program after bad press. You know what I am talking about, right? A manager or executive (or several) is called out on their conduct. You fear lawsuits and bad press, so you hurry to implement a program to stop the bleeding. This is reactive. Employees, suppliers, consumers — the world — will see this as a superficial, performative DEIB program. It doesn't have staying power.

Finally, you can't have trust and transparency without communication. Diversity means different things to different people. A failure to communicate short and long-term DEIB goals leave everyone guessing. You have to define what DEIB is to the organization, what you hope to get and GIVE from your DEIB efforts, and then continue to keep the open and consistent dialog on the subject.

Lack of Support

DEIB efforts need support from all directions and in different ways. Perhaps, this sounds like just another obvious statement, but missing links in the area of support are consistent when efforts fail.

First, key leaders often lack the courage to deal with the resistance to DEIB in the organization. Notice I say KEY leaders — not just C-Suite. Think of leaders both horizontally and vertically through the organization. You could have extraordinary support at the top, but if you have one lower-level manager not on board, you have one bad apple spoiling the cart. You are only as strong as the weakest link.

There is often resistance to change — any kind of change. But when talking about a cultural shift and DEIB, there is sometimes a dimension of insecurity and uncertainty that needs addressing. If you are a primarily homogenous workforce, employees have all kinds of fears and questions. Are jobs at stake? What will happen with pay? Will my words be taken out of context? How does this impact my environment? If there is a feeling that it is a reactive and performative initiative, eye rolls and noncompliance will follow.

Second, you can have an entire program collapse before it gets off the ground if it isn't backed by a budget and transparent policies and procedures that have strong backing. You can't have one and not the other. Sure, you need a budget for DEIB training, but you should also consider a budget for promotion, recruiting and hiring, and fair and equitable pay to name a few. Will you have money to cultivate culture and belonging? Things like team building, guest speakers, or community partnerships are not always free. There is no commitment without a budget.

Finally, you HAVE to change your policies and procedures to promote DEIB. You need to memorialize your DEIB framework and processes. It goes back to communication. How will your DEIB program succeed if the expectations are unclear? How will you hold people accountable or your organization responsible for the effort? If you want your policies and procedures to reflect your commitment, you must review them and make sure the dots connect.

Whom will you have to review your policies and procedures to ensure they gel with the DEIB strategy and commitments you want to make? Will it be HR, an attorney, or a DEIB expert?

You will get three different results! One will focus on protecting the company from complaints. One will focus on protecting the company from getting sued. And one will focus on creating an environment where you don't have to worry about the other two!

Lack of Action

When we talk of action, there are the reactive and the proactive. The reactive is the performative DEIB program implemented out of fear and what seems like a necessity. You don't want your action to be reactive. You want to be ahead of the curve — be proactive. You want your DEIB actions to support a sense of belonging. After all, that is the ultimate end goal. Places where action fails are creating awareness but no sustainable actions or activities, implicit bias going unchecked, and inadequate training.

An idea not acted on is still only an idea. A DEIB effort takes — effort. Effort equals action. You may have daily, weekly, or quarterly conversations about DEIB that bring awareness, but those don't convert to action. You must put your money where your mouth is — walk the walk. If you say you plan to review pay equality and right the ship, do you have the budget to do that? Is it sustainable? Or did you make a statement that you are aware of pay inequality, but it's out of your hands? See the disconnect?

Then there is the implicit (or unconscious) bias that goes unchecked. So often, organizations don't want to touch on the uncomfortable subject that we all have bias. Yet, if you gloss over this subject, your DEIB will surely experience setbacks, if not failure.

We all fall victim to our underlying bias — those stereotypes that have been engrained into our DNA. Of course, we know the most egregious. For example, the white woman who will clutch her purse as she walks past a Black man on the sidewalk. But there are so many other more subtle examples that have an impact. Did you know that author Malcolm Gladwell randomly sampled male CEOs and found that 33% were 6 foot 2 inches tall or taller? He believes we have an unconscious bias that "height correlates to success."[21] A Chinese study also found that taller

---

[21] https://online.maryville.edu/blog/addressing-implicit-bias/

people made more money. Others include assuming 'all Asian people are good at math' or assuming a person with a disability will take more sick time from work. You get the point.

That brings us to training. First, training has to include addressing implicit bias. If it doesn't, you are missing the boat. From there, DEIB training needs to be experiential. Most DEIB training fails because it is dry, rout memorization with no emotional or logical connection to what is going on in your organization, culture, or with your employees. Watching videos and clicking through a multiple choice test at the end only breeds resentment. For the homogenous groups, it is a waste of time and just a way for HR to cover their backside. It is a waste of time for the underrepresented because it doesn't foster change.

Traditional training is pre-packaged and doesn't give the tools and strategies to apply what is learned in the actual work environment. Employees need to know how to connect the pieces. We learn by doing — through experimenting, not sitting in front of a video or presentation for two hours.

I am sure you have been through your share of pointless videos and multiple-choice tests — how did you like them? Enough said! The problem is that we have trained to the same videos and been talked at for so long that there are now myths and misconceptions about DEIB. They are worth noting for perspective.

Myths and Misconceptions

Myth 1: Diversity only favors minorities and women.

This is one of the most pervasive myths; thus, it is crucial to dispel it and make people aware that taking action to promote diversity and equality has global benefits. Remember, diversity includes veterans, people with disabilities, LGBTQ+, the neurodiverse, those from different religions or socioeconomic backgrounds, and so much more. Painting diversity in broad brush strokes to favor more people from other historically underrepresented groups is advantageous for the entire ecosystem. Financially, companies with greater gender equality in their executive teams have a 21% higher likelihood of experiencing better profitability than businesses with less gender equality. Further, companies with executive teams that are ethnically and culturally diverse are 33% more likely to be industry leaders in profitability.

Myth 2: Women or minorities can't occupy certain positions.

Women are still underrepresented in the labor market because of their late entry into the workforce. Historically, both they and minorities have been able to enter professions with fewer qualifications. The claim that there aren't enough qualified women of color to fill highly specialized roles or management committees is one of the most frequently claimed justifications for excluding minority women from those roles.

It appears natural to assume that the balance will eventually swing if we look at the data on women attending the university and graduate women because they outnumber the male student population in many nations. However, in the meantime, we must work to guarantee that, above all, diverse candidates are always presented in the selection, promotion, and succession processes.

Myth 3: The primary means of achieving inclusion are quotas.

Another of the finest discussions on the subject is the application of meritocracy or quotas. Because they serve as an accelerator, gender quotas can be beneficial and successful. On the whole, though, they are not the most effective strategy for integrating minorities and women. We repeatedly see that quotas alone do not work, and candidates must possess the necessary skills in addition to belonging to a group or an underrepresented minority.

It would be more practical for companies to create a work culture with objectives and recognition based on results—where profiles highlight a person's expertise rather than their gender or ethnicity. Yet, this is often easier said than done. The reality is that as a result of the slow pace of change, quotas are a mechanism that gains more ground every day even though we know it will not bring about the profound changes required to transform culture.

Myth 4: HR is in charge of the equity plan.

The problem is that HR can't do it alone. The success of implementing an equity strategy depends on senior management's commitment. It would be best if you were on board with the goal, believe in the advantages it will bring about, and support and encourage it. It can only succeed if it is regarded as a company priority. If not, little incremental improvements will be made, but rarely any real advancement.

Furthermore, everyone in management should be involved. Every employee, regardless of category, function, or department, must adopt the required attitudes and behaviors in their sphere of influence to ensure the success of equality.

Many initiatives fail because women start them for women; they are not evaluated with objective facts. They lack the motivation of the management committee, or men in the company believe that the issue does not affect them.

Myth 5: White men aren't included in diversity.

Some might believe that diversity initiatives exclude or ignore white men, but this is a misconception. Diversity is about recognizing and valuing the broad spectrum of human differences, which includes race, gender, age, and more. White men, like anyone else, benefit from and contribute to a diverse environment. The aim of DEIB initiatives is to foster an inclusive culture where everyone—regardless of their background—feels valued and has an opportunity to thrive. By embracing diversity, organizations can harness a wide range of perspectives, including those of white men, to drive innovation and success. The focus is not on excluding anyone but on creating a more inclusive and equitable environment for all.

Myth 6: Diversity is not required.

Many people might feel that diversity initiatives are not essential or are merely a "nice-to-have" rather than a necessity. In reality, diversity is crucial for fostering innovation, improving decision-making, and enhancing overall organizational performance. Diverse teams bring a range of perspectives, which can lead to more creative solutions and better problem-solving.

For example, a team that includes individuals from various backgrounds, experiences, and viewpoints is more likely to anticipate and address the needs of a diverse customer base. This can lead to more effective marketing strategies, product designs, and customer service approaches. Embracing diversity isn't just about meeting a requirement; it's about enhancing the effectiveness and competitiveness of the organization.

Myth 7: DEIB is just about handouts, not merit.

It's a common misconception that Diversity, Equity, Inclusion, and Belonging (DEIB) initiatives undermine meritocracy by focusing on giving handouts rather than rewarding skill and achievement. In reality, DEIB aims to create systematic processes and procedures ensuring equitable opportunities for all, including in interviewing and hiring, promotion, performance appraisals, and professional development.

The goal is to establish a level playing field where everyone has the opportunity to showcase their talents and contributions. DEIB efforts are designed to remove barriers that might prevent talented individuals from reaching their potential due to biases or systemic inequalities. By addressing these barriers, we're not diminishing merit but ensuring that merit is the true measure of success for everyone.

Myth 8: DEIB creates division and is politically motivated.

Some believe that DEIB is a tool for creating division or is driven by a specific political agenda. In truth, DEIB is about fostering a workplace where every employee feels valued and can contribute their best work. It's not about dividing people but about bridging gaps and ensuring that everyone has the opportunity to succeed. DEIB initiatives are grounded in principles of fairness and respect, not politics. They are designed to create a more inclusive environment that benefits all employees by promoting understanding and collaboration across diverse backgrounds.

Myth 9: DEIB is reverse discrimination.

A common myth is that DEIB programs are a form of reverse discrimination, unfairly favoring certain groups over others. In reality, DEIB initiatives aim to level the playing field, not tip it in one direction. The goal is to address historical and systemic disadvantages that have impacted various groups, ensuring everyone has a fair chance to succeed.

For example, employees with disabilities might need accommodations like accessible workspaces or assistive technologies, which aren't about giving them an unfair advantage but about ensuring they can perform their job effectively. Veterans may require specialized training programs to transition smoothly into civilian roles, helping them bridge gaps in skills and experience.

A neurodiverse employee might benefit from flexible work hours or a quieter workspace to enhance their productivity. Individuals for whom English is a second language might benefit from translation services or language support to ensure they fully understand and engage with workplace materials and communications. Far from being about reverse discrimination, DEIB is about fairness and creating opportunities for all by recognizing and addressing these existing disparities in the workplace.

Myth 10: Equity and equality are the same thing.

Another misconception is that equity and equality are interchangeable concepts. While they might seem similar, they are fundamentally different. Equality means treating everyone the same way, regardless of their starting point. For example, offering the same amount of time off to all employees, without considering individual needs, might not address the unique circumstances of each person. Equity involves recognizing that different people have different needs and providing support to ensure everyone has an opportunity to succeed. For instance, some employees may need additional time off for maternal or paternal leave, while others might require time to care for an elderly parent or recover from surgery. DEIB focuses on equity because it acknowledges that treating everyone the same doesn't always result in fair outcomes, and it aims to address those underlying differences to achieve true fairness.

Myth 11: DEIB is a waste of time and not a necessary requirement.

Some might argue that DEIB initiatives are a waste of time or an unnecessary burden. However, the truth is that DEIB is crucial for creating a thriving, innovative, and productive workplace. Diverse teams bring a variety of perspectives and ideas, leading to better problem-solving and decision-making. Initiatives rooted in DEIB, such as implementing comprehensive mentorship programs, creating employee resource groups, and ensuring equitable career development opportunities, contribute to a culture of belonging. For example, mentorship programs can help underrepresented employees navigate their careers and build connections, while employee resource groups provide a supportive community and a platform for diverse voices.

Creating equitable career development opportunities ensures that all employees have access to the resources and support they need to advance. These efforts not only enhance productivity and retention but also help organizations achieve recognition as top employers. Far from being a waste of time, DEIB is a strategic imperative that drives business success by fostering an environment where all employees feel valued and empowered to contribute their best.

Myth 12: DEIB initiatives are only for large organizations.

Some believe that DEIB efforts are only necessary for large corporations. However, DEIB is valuable for organizations of all sizes. Regardless of the organization's size, fostering an inclusive environment can enhance employee satisfaction, improve retention, and drive innovation. For instance, small businesses can benefit from DEIB by building a strong, supportive culture that attracts diverse talent and increases employee engagement. Implementing initiatives like inclusive hiring practices, flexible work arrangements, and diversity training can help create a positive and equitable workplace culture.

Mid-sized organizations can see similar benefits, such as improved team collaboration and creativity, by leveraging DEIB to bring in diverse perspectives and address any systemic biases. No matter the size, organizations that prioritize DEIB are better positioned to thrive in today's competitive market and create a workplace where all employees feel valued and empowered. Far from being a luxury reserved for the big players, DEIB is a strategic advantage that supports organizational success across the board.

Myth 13: DEIB is a one-time initiative.

A common misconception is that DEIB is a one-time project or checklist. In reality, DEIB is an ongoing journey that requires continuous effort, evaluation, and adjustment. Embedding DEIB into the DNA of an organization means integrating these principles into every aspect of operations and culture. For example, an organization that consistently revisits and updates its DEIB strategies might implement regular training sessions, conduct annual reviews of its inclusivity practices, and establish employee resource groups that address emerging issues.

A company that truly commits to DEIB will adapt its hiring practices to ensure they reflect a diverse candidate pool, regularly measure progress using metrics like employee satisfaction and retention rates, and foster an environment where feedback on inclusivity is actively sought and acted upon. By making DEIB a fundamental part of the organization's values and operations, businesses can enjoy long-term benefits such as enhanced employee morale, increased innovation, and a stronger reputation as an employer of choice. Far from being a checkbox, DEIB is a continuous effort that drives sustained success and meaningful change.

Myth 14: DEIB efforts are just about being politically correct.

Some might view DEIB as merely a matter of political correctness. However, DEIB is far more than just surface-level politeness; it involves making substantive changes to policies, practices, and attitudes that foster genuine respect and inclusion. Regardless of political perspective—whether conservative, democrat, libertarian, or independent—the core values of DEIB resonate universally. We all strive for fairness, the ability to be rewarded for our work, opportunities to excel based on our talents and work ethic, and a system where meritocracy prevails. DEIB efforts aim to ensure accommodations for those who need them, such as providing flexible work arrangements for parents or accessible facilities for people with disabilities. By focusing on these fundamental goals, DEIB helps create a workplace where everyone can contribute their best and feel valued. It's not just about adhering to political trends; it's about fostering a truly equitable and inclusive environment that benefits everyone.

Barriers to DEIB

We often interchange barriers to DEIB with why DEIB efforts fail. In some instances, they overlap. For example, if you lack support with resistance from crucial leaders or no budget, those are clear barriers. However, other variables can doom your DEIB efforts before you even begin. Failed programs are closely tied to these barriers.

We have already touched on the importance of leadership support. But before that, you have to have leadership buy-in. If you don't have the buy-in, you won't have the support when you later implement your initiatives—getting buy-in and support are not the same. Buy-in is the active willingness to participate. It is the agreement to support your efforts actively and positively. At the same time, leaders can give support without buy-in. For example, let's say you are a firefighter. Your unconscious bias may tell you that women shouldn't be firefighters. You don't believe they have the physical strength to do the job. However, you won't stop them from applying for the job. If they get hired, you offer to assist them just like all other new recruits. Yet, your support isn't active or positive. Maybe you watch this woman struggle and mumble that you saw it coming or only help if she asks for it.

Now, take that same scenario with buy-in AND support. You believe that women can do the job just as well as men. You encourage women applicants. You hire a woman and then see that the struggles she works through are no different from other new recruits. You and the others jump in and bring her into the fold. You offer guidance and tips or tricks before she even asks.

See the difference? Now expand that personal bias and resistance to the broader culture. Cultural resistance is the above scenario amplified. Unconscious bias and cultural resistance are the most significant barriers to overcome. It will take a concerted effort to put all the pieces in place to overcome this hurdle.

That brings up the next barrier to DEIB — the lack of planning. Unfortunately, DEIB can't be an out-of-the-box solution where you buy a license to a few videos and take some suggestions about team-building exercises. Every organization is unique. Every organizational culture is different. There isn't a 'one size fits all DEIB package. I know, I know — due to budget restrictions, you have no choice.

And — now that you mention it! That brings us to the next two barriers. Inexperience and budget restrictions. These two go hand in hand. If you have inexperienced staff and couple that with budget restrictions, your DEIB efforts will fall flat. You are back to organizational resentment over watching DEIB videos once a year. You can't work from a 'check the box and be done with it' strategy. But we do this because this is what we have always done.

Historically, there is a very one-dimensional argument against DEIB efforts — we can't afford it. We can't afford training. We can't afford to hire an expert — we can't afford to set budget aside for pay, or hiring, or promotion, or . . . pick your poison. Am I right? Without a budget, you get inexperienced staff and inadequate training.

In most cases, DEIB is just another project dumped in HR's lap. HR now has to carry their normal workload while being told they now have to find or make time to build a DEIB program. Talk about creating a culture of resentment from the get-go. If HR starts from the point of resentment, how do you think this will flow from there? HR will roll out with the "you have to do this because it is an HR requirement" instead of a more positive jumping-off point.

That brings us to the next issue. Perhaps the biggest barrier to DEIB getting off the ground is the lack of an all-encompassing, comprehensive, and strategic DEIB plan. Most plans lack specific goals and metrics, inconsistent messaging or communication, and an inability to sell the business case for DEIB internally.

Think about it for a second. You get everyone at the top nodding their heads in agreement — yes, we need a DEIB program. You get a budget and then spread the word that you are focused on diversity. And? What goals do you hope to accomplish? How will you measure your goals? For example, you understand that you want everyone to have a sense of belonging, but what does that look like? How do you know people feel like they belong? What resources are you providing across the organization?

Take another example. Say you want to increase diversity in leadership. Are you focused on women in leadership, BIPOC, the LGBTQ+ community, veterans, individuals with disabilities, the neurodiverse, or all of the above? What do you expect the results to be when you shift focus to increasing diversity in leadership? Is that goal being communicated consistently, and does everybody from the top down know and understand what's in it for them?

When you sell the business case for diversity, you aren't just trying to sell it to shareholders. You must sell it to the employees, the managers, and the suppliers. For each group, the sell may look slightly different. For shareholders, it is about the bottom line. For employees, it is about belonging and boosting employee satisfaction and confidence. For suppliers, it's about equitable and profitable contract opportunities.

So how do you overcome these barriers?

Overcoming Barriers

We all confront obstacles when trying to reach goals. Think about your personal goals. How did you overcome barriers when you wanted to eat healthier or lose weight? It didn't happen overnight. Your excess weight and unhealthy habits took years to embed in your lifestyle. This is no different—the organizational culture developed over the years. The key is that you have to start somewhere and take the first step.

Think about the first steps you took when making a lifestyle change. I would guess you had to change your mindset. You have to be able to see the end result and the benefits you will enjoy. You had to stay accountable to your goals and needed support, right? So, you buy the running shoes, throw out the junk food, and block out thirty minutes every other day to exercise. You learn new recipes and read about proper nutrition and workouts. You go to the gym, take a beginner's class, and then move to an intermediate class. Maybe you get a mentor, hire an accountability partner who is a coach, yoga instructor, or personal trainer, or ask your significant other to support you.

You measure progress by counting calories, weighing yourself every week, and taking body measurements. After a while, your consistency pays off. One day you run into someone you haven't seen for a year, and they mention how good you look — *hey, you look good! Did you lose weight?*

Treat your commitment to DEIB and overcoming barriers as you would your personal goals. Integrate DEIB activities and effort into the daily culture — the daily routine. You won't see results immediately, but you can track the small changes that begin to happen. Celebrate the small successes just as you would when you complete your first 5k run. Be sure you prioritize education and promote cross-level collaboration — find the cheerleaders and mentors. Hire that coach or trainer (the DEIB expert) to guide and hold you accountable. Just like with exercise, we need someone to give us the carrot or the stick! Finally, stick with it! It takes concerted effort that is consistent over time.

If you made the connection, you might think — *okay, I get it now. But where can I start? What does that first step look like?*

Across the board, some best practices work regardless of culture, the industry, or where the initiatives come from. These are the proven best practices.

DEIB Best Practices

Every best effort **begins with authenticity** and **starts with a plan**. It doesn't have to be extravagant or complicated, but it needs to be authentic. You can't just organize a one-off event like videos once a year and call it good. These one-off events will be viewed as insincere. Remember, the workforce isn't naive. Your plan should be unique to your culture.

To build a better DEIB plan, we first need to rethink where our DEIB plan starts. In most cases, the human resources department creates the initiative. The problem then lies in the fact that most HR departments are working from a position of risk avoidance. A DEIB program is to avoid being sued by disgruntled employees and ensure employees maintain a certain level of productivity and efficiency for the company, right? Maybe not all the time, but generally, it is not about creating a sense of belonging.

A better or BEST practice would be to connect your DEIB to environmental, social, and governance strategy (ESG). If you aren't sure, consider this. A recent CNBC survey revealed that "a huge majority of the workforce (78%) says it is important to them to work at an organization that priorities diversity and inclusion, and in fact more than half (53%) consider it to be 'very important' to them."[22]

Your ESG and DEIB strategies go hand in hand. Further, there is a strong argument that connecting your DEIB to ESG will strengthen each component of your ESG efforts.[23] In the Global Diversity Practice article, *Diversity and Inclusion Are More Than the 'S' in ESG*; they say how DEI supports better ESG efforts:

---

[22] https://www.surveymonkey.com/curiosity/cnbc-workforce-survey-april-2021/
[23] https://globaldiversitypractice.com/diversity-and-inclusion-are-more-than-the-s-in-esg/

- **Environmental** - A diverse pool of employees is more likely to be aware of how environmental issues affect different areas and communities, which enables the business to introduce strategies that reflect local needs. In-depth, first-hand knowledge is vital when designing innovative solutions for reducing a business's carbon footprint.

- **Social** - This aspect of ESG focuses on how a company manages its internal and external relationships. It looks at work conditions, health and safety, and diversity. Companies that actively recruit people from a range of ethnic and social backgrounds score high in this area of ESG.

   Research shows that 35% of employees' emotional investment in their work and 20% of their desire to stay within their existing company is down to how included they feel in their workplace. Therefore, D&I undoubtedly results in more loyal, hard-working, and dedicated employees.

- **Governance** - This examines executive decision-making and leadership style. It considers factors such as equal pay, equal opportunities, and potential corruption. Inequality and ethical leadership behavior underline every D&I strategy. Employees -and other stakeholders- know they can voice their concerns and that problems are quickly dealt with.

   Repeated research has shown that gender-diverse boards are linked to improved investment efficiency, better engagement between board members, and fewer fraud cases and operations-based lawsuits. The inclusion of women on corporate boards also increases the likelihoods of discussion on social issues, climate change, and work/life balance."

Perhaps the pieces are beginning to fit together? You're convinced but not sure where to start. The best practice is to engage and ask!

Engage and Ask

But how do you make that happen? You should **engage the entire organization**. You want input and buy-in from executives, employees, suppliers, and external stakeholders. When you engage everyone from top to bottom and vertically, you will have a better-formulated plan and show a genuine interest in inclusion and belonging. After all, what better way to bring everyone together and build an inclusive culture than engaging from the get-go?! This one act is the beginning of a beautiful relationship and creates a feedback loop that is desperately needed yet overlooked.

When we ask questions, it is a way to show interest. Further, when we ask for help, it is human nature to want to help. Several studies tell us we are motivated to help others. For example, when someone does something nice for us, we feel inclined to do something nice in return. If we see someone do something nice for someone, it often motivates us to do something nice. We also know that doing something nice for someone makes us feel good. So, if we are in the process of doing something nice and asking for help, the chances are you will get assistance. So, **ASK** what your people need or want to feel a sense of belonging. If that is too open-ended, start with asking about holidays.

Of course, we have to be careful not to violate the laws but consider asking about **what holidays or cultural celebrations employees want to see recognized**. Then let them lead the path forward on the subject and how to integrate these special days. Now, I know what you are thinking. This means we will have to take days off or close shop for every single holiday imaginable.

That just simply isn't the case. You can consider floating holidays instead of everyone getting Christmas Day off.

Further, not every holiday is a day off. Some people just want acknowledgment. So, a sense of belonging could be as simple as adding a multicultural calendar to display.

You want to **switch from operating from cultural fit to cultural contribution**. But what does that mean? Consider your current culture and hiring practices. Do decision-makers ever send apology letters to candidates that say, "we didn't feel you were the right fit." Maybe you didn't put it in writing but said it or thought it. Think about that for a second. You are looking to fit someone into the current culture rather than look for that candidate's potential cultural contribution.

Now, I hear it — the mumbles of *I never pass over candidates due to their cultural differences; that's illegal*. I would remind you of the unconscious bias. We don't blatantly pass over candidates (or at least I hope that isn't the case). However, you may interview someone and have a gut feeling that they don't fit in or wouldn't work well with the current team. Why? Maybe they are too serious and analytical, and you have a bunch of free spirits. I would challenge you to ask the candidate what they could contribute to the environment. Let them tell you how they would integrate. You may find that they will bring balance to the team.

Attract and Recruit

For that reason, you want to **attract and recruit diverse talent**. Keep an open mind and implement unbiased recruiting practices. You can do this in many ways. First, you must **look at your job descriptions** when attracting diverse talent. We often have **discriminatory language lurking** there and never realize it. For example, women are often deterred from jobs asking for a "ninja" or "rockstar." They are also less likely to apply for jobs unless they meet the qualifications 100%. So, consider softening requirements to "nice to have."

Another good option for diversity hiring is to **implement blind recruitment**. Studies repeatedly show that we make assumptions about names. Blind recruitment is a process by which personal identifying information is removed from resumes. This will remove the unconscious bias and discrimination up front.

Of course, there are hundreds of other ways to attract and recruit diverse talent from opt-in talent networks for candidates, social media, and even where you post jobs or places you recruit from. The point is to start somewhere. It doesn't have to cost a fortune. Remember, it just needs to be genuine and have a consistent flow from attracting and recruiting to onboarding, retaining, and offboarding.

Onboarding

So, you are excited because you have attracted and recruited some diverse talent. Now what?

Well, if you haven't heard, most onboarding processes are awful to begin with, let alone when trying to integrate DEIB. So, use your pursuit of DEIB to upgrade your onboarding process. Onboarding isn't (or shouldn't be) about filling out paperwork, getting badges, and being escorted to the bathroom and coffee pot. Although, the bathroom location is essential for employees working in the office. It is your opportunity to create a story — and a meaningful experience that your new recruit will never forget!

Think about it. How do we feel about that first day on the job? Often it is overwhelming. Ask someone, how was your first day — what do you get? Did you know that employees who experience negative onboarding are more likely to look for other job opportunities, while great onboarding can improve retention? If employees have a great first day or first week, they are more likely to try and recruit their network of friends or past coworkers. Onboarding then amplifies its purpose and becomes a recruiting tool.

Let's break onboarding down into four crucial stages: Compliance, Contribution, Culture, and Connection.

- **Compliance** - This is where you lay down the rules and policies of the organization, along with all the necessary paperwork. But don't let it stop there – use this as an opportunity to set the stage for what's to come.

- **Contribution** - This is where you introduce employees to their roles and responsibilities. Describe upcoming projects they'll be involved in and how they can contribute.

Make them feel like they're an integral part of the team right from the get-go.

- **Culture** - This is where you explain the norms of the organization. Give them a tour of the facilities (if applicable), describe how things work, and show them how they fit within and impact the larger organization. And don't forget to discuss DEI initiatives – make it clear that your organization is committed to creating a culture of inclusion and belonging.

- **Connection**. This is where a new employee starts to feel like part of the team. Introduce them to as many of their coworkers as possible, encourage team members to include them in formal and informal activities, and assign a mentor or buddy who can bridge the gap between the new employee and their coworkers. Provide resources, like information on Employee Resource Groups, to help foster connections.

In what ways can you improve onboarding to integrate DEIB? Do you facilitate and introduce recruits to ongoing training opportunities or resource groups? Do you take the time to open the feedback loop and ask questions about personal preferences and emphasize the desire to create a sense of belonging? Or do you dictate and direct?

Finally, offboarding can be as important as onboarding. Of course, we never like it when someone leaves, but we always want to take the opportunity to hear why. Offboarding is a way to seek opportunities to improve. I know — you assume they left for more money or advancement. But not always. Then you think — nobody ever participates or lies, which is a wasted exercise.

I would argue that you aren't doing it right. Your offboarding focuses on YOU. How will you transfer knowledge, how will you finish projects, and now you have to interview for a replacement? But here's the thing. If you know that about every four years that position will come open, then perhaps it is worth focusing on what to do for retention and recruitment.

Consider the facts. Harvard Business Review reported in 2021 that employees might pay more attention to how we end an employment relationship than how we start them. The argument is weighted heavily on research completed by behavioral scientist and Noble laureate Daniel Kahneman where he introduces the "peak-end rule."[24] He suggests that we will more often judge events based on the most intense point and the end rather than the entire experience as a whole. With that, your offboarding should begin when you onboard. Let new employees know that you hope they stay, but there are resources through their time with you, including if they decide to part ways for other opportunities.

Yes, it sounds counterintuitive and perhaps hard to wrap your head around. Why in the world would you discuss their departure? Turnover is a bad word. Yet, bringing it up openly so they can see you care for the person coming and going shows authenticity. Most organizations have a large percentage of employees who will stay in contact with others after leaving. If you build a positive alumni network, you create more opportunities to recruit from that network. If the network is diverse — two birds, one stone! It's about employee investment.

---

[24] https://hbr.org/2021/03/turn-departing-employees-into-loyal-alumni

Employee Investment

With onboarding and offboarding as the book ends, we now need to consider the content in between. From start to end, what can we provide employees to support and even enhance DEIB engagement and efforts consistently? One of the most significant ways to keep DEIB at the forefront is through personal development, training, mentoring, coaching, education assistance, and even cross-department shadowing. These activities integrate diverse perspectives from traditional aspects like race, gender, and culture. It opens the DEIB feedback loop and lines of communication from micro-culture to micro-culture within the organization.

You become more transparent when you crack the internal barriers to these microcosmic cultures. You can reshape your internal and external communications to better align with your overarching DEIB values and goals. This transparency also opens the gate for other avenues to implement equitable policies, allow for increased accountability, and have real-time data to measure your DEIB efforts.

Now, let's talk about the elephant in the room — pay and benefits.

"I suppose I'll be the one to mention the elephant in the room."

Did you know that a PwC survey revealed that 65% of employees are job hunting because they want better pay?[25] Now, this doesn't mean that you have to increase wages immediately. However, you should be doing your research to see what the competition is offering. If they provide higher base wages and you can't budget for that right now, consider bonus programs or more attractive benefit options. Whatever you do, you have to ensure that you have fair and equitable pay practices. Word gets out. Employees talk. And now, some states require that pay for positions be disclosed. So, there is no hiding.

Remember the theme — transparency, and authenticity. If you have a pay equity problem, acknowledge it and then have a plan to fix it. If you can't raise wages right now to match the competition, perhaps you offer performance bonuses or attractive alternative benefits like additional paid days off (the four-day work week, anyone?). Maybe you provide better advancement or promotion opportunities.

Finally, consider your other policies and practices. From accessibility and disciplinary policies to interviewing practices and performance reviews, take inventory. Can you answer yes to the following:

- It is fair and equitable
- It is transparent
- It is authentic
- It is employee focused (for the benefit of)
- Employees want it

---

[25] https://www.forbes.com/sites/square/2021/09/28/how-to-make-long-term-investments-in-your-staff/?sh=7fa74c8771aa

- Employees suggested it
- It is competitive with or better than the industry standard

If you can't answer yes, you need to go back and reevaluate the purpose of what it is you are offering.

Now let's shift gears slightly. Most everything we have touched on up to now has been focused internally. Yet, a holistic DEIB program will be all-encompassing. You must incorporate your suppliers or vendors (which we will call suppliers for brevity) and external help (the DEIB expert – shameless plug).

Let's address the diversity of the supplier base first.

Supplier Based Diversity (SBD)

Supplier Based Diversity falls under the corporate social responsibility (CSR) umbrella. SBD is the practice of including smaller and diverse-owned supplier businesses within your supply chain. When you incorporate these small to medium-sized diverse businesses into your supply chain, you help local economies where they are located. You are encouraging job creation which in turn increases consumption and spending in the area around the diverse business. Further, you are extending the reach of your DEIB efforts by being a role model to the supplier. You can encourage their DEIB practices and be a change maker within that community. And don't forget that DEIB promotes innovation. So, you could see your supplier branch out into new markets or innovate a new solution for your business.

SBD is a win/win for you and your supplier. For your organization, you are extending the reach of your DEIB program and thereby building your ethical reputation. For the diverse supplier, you are increasing their profitability, innovation, employee satisfaction, and community standing as a contributor to the local economy.

Maybe you are already convinced that procurement of diverse suppliers can increase your DEIB. However, you are either unsure how to go about it or have had challenges implementing DEIB in supplier procurement. Here are a few best practices to overcome the barriers and implement a strong, diverse supplier procurement program:

- Register with trade organizations and nonprofits that can help connect your organization to diverse suppliers. Two of the most prominent are the National Minority Supplier Diversity Council and Women's Business Enterprise National Council. Each has regional affiliates with connections to local and independent networks that promote supplier diversity.

- Promote your supplier diversity procurement efforts. First, publicize your interest and efforts with your current suppliers and the nonprofits or trade organizations. When you make your current vendors aware of your efforts, you might be surprised by the momentum it can create. If you have only one minority-owned vendor, reach out. Most assuredly, they know of other diverse business owners and are often happy to make the connections for you. From there, word can get out, and you can leverage your diverse supplier contacts to increase your efforts to benefit everyone.

The DEIB Expert

No, really — we need to talk about it. I can give you all the tips and tricks from here to the moon, but knowledge and application are two different things. You don't know what you don't know. You are an expert at the thing you do. You spend hundreds or thousands of hours perfecting your skills. You know what you do inside and out. But you can't be expected to wear all hats and be all things to all people. Also, consider that you and everyone in the organization have an underlying bias. You don't know it because you are in the bubble, but it is there.

Think about your house. Do you know what it smells like? Now think about when you go on vacation and come home. You open the front door, and there is an odor. Not necessarily a bad odor — just an odor. It smells like home. Although, if you forgot to empty the trash, it could smell like a dumpster (not that I know). Now, think about going to a friend's or family member's house. They greet you and invite you in. Their home has a smell. Maybe good, maybe not. You mention the smell, and your friend has no idea what you are talking about. The thing is, we never notice how our home smells — unless we have been away for a while.

Our bias is the same way. We often can't recognize our bias because we live with it daily. It takes an outsider to point it out. It takes an outsider to bring awareness to the culture and habits we have created.

A DEIB expert will help you analyze and measure your current culture and DEIB efforts by surveying employees and identifying gaps. The right expert will look at everything from images and language on websites, social media, and boards to job descriptions and policies. Then, they will help create a feedback loop, get buy-in, set goals and help you implement a DEIB program that is as deep as it is wide. The goal is to have your DEIB efforts going 24/7/365.

When fully integrated, you should expect a program that includes consistent awareness with training, content, and conversations that incorporate company milestones and key teachable moments through news, current events, and constant feedback. Then, your expert will use the feedback loop to help measure what is working or not working and how to pivot appropriately for improvement. Finally, your DEIB expert will be your accountability partner to ensure your organization has the systems and processes to address DEIB issues when they arise appropriately.

Now, some of you reading will say — yeah, this is not new information, we hired a chief diversity office (CDO), and it didn't work out. Nothing changed, so we let them go. Let's address that.

First, the turnover for CDOs is high. Forbes reported in 2021 that:

> *"Many CDOs are set up to fail because they become their company's scapegoat when DEI efforts and initiatives are ineffective. Creating an environment that is safe from harm, inclusive, and built on justice and equity should be every employee's responsibility. CDOs are expected to perform miracles without a team, and with little to no financial support. One person cannot change a toxic work culture."*[26]

So, first, you should ask if everyone was part of the solution or if they contributed to the problem. One person can't change the world. Also, remember the house analogy? The longer the DEIB expert stays, the longer they have to acclimate to the smell, and then it goes unnoticed even by them. Finally, internal CDOs must work through the corporate bureaucracy to try and get things done. In comparison, an external consultant can operate independently of the organization's culture and constructs.

---

[26] https://www.forbes.com/sites/janicegassam/2021/12/29/4-dei-practices-your-company-should-adopt-in-2022/?sh=2de3765041d5

REFLECTION AND APPLICATION

- Consider your business case for implementing a DEIB program. Do you see profitability, innovation, or increased employee satisfaction? Or is it an exercise in CYA?
- If you have or had a DEIB program and it failed, why? Was it budget, buy-in, planning, or?
- What are the barriers to a DEIB program? Cultural resistance, inexperienced staff, budget, or?
- Do you see a path to break through the barriers?
- Could you easily implement some best practices NOW? Which ones?
- How could you involve your supplier base?
- Do you need to involve an expert?

CHAPTER 3

GETTING BUY-IN & COMMITMENT AT ALL LEVELS

> *"If you make the unconditional commitment to reach your most important goals, if the strength of your decision is sufficient, you will find the way and the power to achieve your goals."*
>
> – Robert Conklin

In This Chapter

- Executive and Board Commitment – a Partnership
- DEIB Committee or Council
- DEIB and People Leaders
- Employer and Employee Resources
- External Stakeholders
- Reflection and Application

For a DEIB program to succeed, we need all hands on deck. There has to be accountability at all levels, from the board and C-Suite to managers and people leaders within teams. Your program will only be as strong as your weakest links.

Your program will only be as strong as your weakest links

So, how do we get the buy-in and commitment we need?

It will start with developing cultural competence, training, and managing a multi-generational ecosystem. Starting from this point will help everything else flow, and we can make much better sense of why some things work and some initiatives fall flat, on deaf ears, or even worse—cause conflict.

A great place to begin is looking at the multi-generational dimensions of your organization. There will not be buy-in at any level if you can't see things from generational perspectives. For example, the Baby Boomer generation has worked an entire lifetime believing that hard work and organizational loyalty should mean something and pay off at retirement. Yet, they lived through the WorldCom scandal, where retirement accounts were entirely wiped off the board. Further, they remember the civil rights movement, women's liberation, and 'traditional family values.'

Alternatively, Generation X (the latch key generation) were left to their own devices, raising themselves for the most part. Over half of their parents were divorced, and they didn't have participation trophies or over-scheduled organized sports programs. They generally want to be left alone to figure things out without someone looking over their shoulder. They have a low tolerance for 'collaborative work' or working in groups.

Of course, these are some broad generalizations, but you get the point. When it comes to diversity and DEIB initiatives, the generational differences affect what will work or be accepted. Sometimes we forget that DEIB has layers and learning about and understanding multi-generational differences are one of those layers that almost everything else will stem from.

From there, you can begin to work through the different levels of the organization for buy-in and commitment. Let's work from the top down.

C-Suite Executives and Board of Directors

You need executive commitment and sponsorship early on. They will control the funding, resources, and messaging. If you think you have it — think again! While we live in a world of C-Suite messaging and talking points for increased DEIB, there is an apparent disconnect. The 2021 SmartRecruiters State of Diversity Report has some surprising statistics. Did you know:

- Only 21% of companies have defined diversity hiring strategies, processes, and goals.
- Only 26% have a way to measure progress on DEI hiring goals.

- A negligible 22% of executives have clear DEI interviewing and hiring goals.[27]

The point is that words might be spoken, but often it stops there. So, never assume you already have the buy-in from the top. The C-Suite sets the tone and is the ultimate role model for the DEIB program and its importance. They will ultimately provide higher visibility to DEIB efforts and be the face of change. Further, it is their influence, social capital (Chapter 1), and power that will protect the vulnerable and draw the connection of DEIB to broader organizational goals. In many ways, the C-Suite acts as superheroes.

"The C-Suite acts as superheroes"

So, how do you get the C-Suite to listen and become champions of a DEIB program that is more than lip service? Start by

---

[27] https://corp.smartbrief.com/original/2021/10/why-executive-sponsorship-critical-achieving-di-goals

having them look in the mirror. Literally. SHRM Executive Network reports that,

> "**Women** make up 56 percent of front-line employees but only **29 percent of the C-suite**, according to the Gartner 2021 Leadership Progression and Diversity Survey, which queried 3,500 employees across 24 industries on the topic in February 2021. **Black and Indigenous people** and other people of color (BIPOC) make up 31 percent of front-line workers, but **only 17 percent of the C-suite**."[28]

Further, less than one percent of C-Suite executives of Fortune 500 companies identify as LGBTQ+.

Now, this isn't to say that companies haven't made genuine efforts to increase diversity at the C-Suite level. Many will argue the improvements they have made. Nor are we saying that you should point the finger and say, "you are the problem." The problem is systemic. A quick look in the mirror will allow for reflection. Underrepresented groups need role models, mentors, and champions. Sometimes, it just takes a reality check to give the C-Suite a nudge.

I challenge you to ask your C-Suite executives how they got to where they are now. Did they have access to a good education, family support, financial support, mentors, or internships? Did they have any significant obstacles that stood in their way? Health issues? Cultural or language barriers? Did they work through difficult socioeconomic conditions like food insecurity, poverty, abuse, neglect, or divorce?

---

[28] https://www.shrm.org/executive/resources/articles/pages/evolving-executive-dei-diversity-c-suite.aspx#:~:text=Women%20make%20up%2056%20percent,the%20topic%20in%20February%202021.

Why go through this exercise? Because the answers open a window to the perception of diversity and the world at large.

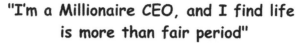

Did you know that socioeconomic status and childhood development play a key role in how risk-averse a CEO will be and how safe they believe the world is? Researchers reveal that social class impacts executive risk-taking behavior, how they handle drastic change, and how secure they see the world around them. The University of Arkansas found that those CEOs raised with wealth and privilege see the world as safer and are often bigger strategic risk takers because they grew up with resources, safety nets, and opportunities.[29] Research from Oregon State University suggests that CEOs from lower status are better

---

[29] https://www.ehstoday.com/safety-leadership/article/21917364/study-examines-relationship-between-ceos-social-class-and-risk-taking

equipped to handle sudden or drastic change due to experiencing adversity in adolescence.[30]

Interestingly, those CEOs who reported to come from the working class to average or middle-class backgrounds tend to be less inclined to take risks or support labor-friendly policies. A study by Henrik Cronqvist from the University of Miami found that CEOs from working or middle-class families tend "to tolerate ungenerous corporate behavior" because that is what they knew growing up as "occupational norms."[31] However, there is a shift happening. The study revealed that younger CEOs are "less stratified with respect to their labor policies; their socioeconomic backgrounds matter less."

So, does the C-Suite see the world as safe, or are they ready, willing, and equipped to take on the changes needed for the DEIB program to be successful?

Now, apply everything that has been laid out to the Board of Directors. Frankly, many in the C-Suite are also on the board — not always, but there is often some overlap. With that said, the Board is ultimately where the buck stops. They are bound by a duty of care and loyalty to the organization and shareholders. They are the bridge from shareholder and social responsibility to the C-Suite and internal processes and management. Therefore, they should offer the overall DEIB vision and oversight so the program will flow seamlessly.

There are some additional questions the Board should consider. Spencer Stuart suggests the following[32]:

---

[30] https://ir.library.oregonstate.edu/downloads/n583z244j
[31] https://hbr.org/2020/07/ceos-from-working-class-families-support-less-labor-friendly-policies
[32] https://www.spencerstuart.com/research-and-insight/corporate-dei-oversight-six-questions-for-boardssocioeconmic%20status

- Should, or will, the DEIB effort fall under an existing committee or part of the environmental, social, and governance (ESG) umbrella?
- How does the board define diversity?
- Does the Board have internal data on the diversity of their organizational workforce, pay structure, and hiring practices? You need to be able to set benchmarks.
- What will you publicly disclose about your workforce diversity?
- Does your succession plan incorporate DEIB goals?

Finally, because the C-Suite and Board are so closely integrated at the top, a partnership must exist between the CEO and the Chairman. This isn't to say they always have to agree; discourse and disagreement often lead to better solutions. However, they have to have the same goals and vision in mind. These two positions are the glue that holds an authentic and transparent DEIB effort together. They also provide the open line of communication needed to cross the distance and gaps between all stakeholders.

When the Board and C-Suite are on the same page, the organization can work through the organizational structure. There are ways the C-Suite and Board can independently promote DEIB while supporting the same vision. Often, this will include creating a DEIB Committee or Council. However, there are other things to consider as well.

How C-Suite Executives Can Promote DEIB at Work

Know that the success of these initiatives will ultimately depend on whether the company has "buy-in" from employees at every level. Especially C-level executives like you if leaders in your organization have chosen to pursue diversity, equity, and inclusion efforts to promote necessary cultural changes in your workplace environment. Here are five ways the whole C-suite, including CEOs, CIOs, COOs, CHROs, and CFOs, can "steer the ship" as their companies travel through the DEIB waters.

Be "The Face" of a Company's DEIB Initiatives - C-level executives are uniquely positioned to set the tone for the entire organization when announcing new initiatives. Therefore, messages sent directly from a CEO will have far more weight and significance than impersonal reports from Human Resources. To get everyone interested, you may, for instance, include the DEIB activities in your monthly emails to staff members and shareholders and at company meetings by expressing your enthusiasm and passion for these initiatives.

Present the DEIB Business Case - The hiring process may not involve C-level executives, depending on the size of your company. The overwhelming proof that organizations who emphasize DEIB see benefits in the form of greater productivity, earnings, employee engagement, and staff retention may be shown to those in charge of hiring. You might also present the business case for DEIB to the shareholders. They will not only see the ROI in their investments but also feel more secure knowing that your company is making substantial efforts to improve and uphold its standing with the general public.

Interact with DEIB at All Levels - Participating in DEIB-focused discussions and getting feedback from all levels of staff, from interns to leaders, is another crucial step in gaining buy-in from everyone in your organization. This "ground floor" involvement is important because it demonstrates your investment in DEIB initiatives to employees. Additionally, it reveals your readiness to learn from others and adapt as needed to provide an inclusive workplace.

Describe Your Connection to DEIB - Perhaps discrimination has harmed you or someone close to you. Don't be scared to share your story when it's suitable. Create a "safe environment" for people in your organization to share their experiences, even if you have not faced discrimination. Sharing personal DEIB experiences may be beneficial for establishing a relationship with other members of your organization and demonstrating your dedication to supporting DEIB initiatives.

Demonstrate to prospective employees that DEIB in the workplace begins at the top - C-level executives can demonstrate to candidates that DEIB is a priority at the highest levels of the organization as part of diversity talent acquisition activities. One suggestion is to make a "welcome" video for the career page on your organization's website in which you discuss the DEIB initiatives you are working on and your enthusiasm for fostering an inclusive workplace culture. It may be necessary to have direct discussions with candidates about your organization's dedication to DEIB and how they affect the working environment if you work for a smaller company and are personally involved in the hiring process. Making your DEIB message a part of the welcome message throughout the onboarding process will also ensure that new hires hear it straight from you.

Involvement of the Board of Directors in DEIB initiatives

The board of directors of a company acts as a vital foundation. They support the establishment of several organizational pillars that later spread outward like a tree's branches. Numerous organizations have expressed a greater desire over the past year to carry out the necessary diversity, equity, inclusion, and belonging (DEIB) efforts that they must also extend to their board of directors.

Investors, other stakeholders, and a growing number of boards now see monitoring of human capital management and workforce diversity as a board obligation, regardless of whether particular boards in the past saw it as falling under their purview.

Boards of directors are more aware that DEIB improves organizational performance, encourages better decision-making, guards against blind spots during board deliberation, and gives them access to more resources and a wider community. To guide their organizations through a commercial and societal transformation in ways that support sustainability, performance, and value, boards play a crucial role.

An outstanding board is a high-performing team with a common goal to advance the organization's work toward a significant objective. By utilizing a wide range of diversity and the skills of people from all racial, ethnic, sexual orientation, thinking, working, and other backgrounds, including professional experience, high-performing boards can execute at their highest levels. To solve social issues, it is essential to create an environment that appreciates the various group's experiences and incorporates them into the supervision of social impact organizations.

DEIB initiatives must go beyond recruiting to address inclusivity, talent development, and retention. Long-term diversity won't increase much by hiring new employees, particularly if the workplace culture prevents women and members of other underrepresented groups from advancing in the company.

Boards should assess whether talent management policies and procedures support inclusion and diversity or serve to reinforce it. Plans for the pipeline and succession of the board and top management, as well as programs for training and development, sponsorship, mentoring, and emerging leaders' programs, should all involve a diverse range of personnel and adhere to the DEIB principles.

Affinity groups should be able to communicate with management; therefore, boards should be aware of the company culture and determine whether it fosters an environment where employees from diverse backgrounds may succeed.

Here are five actions boards can take to more effectively direct and impact their organizations' strategic and systemic DEIB projects:

1. **Draft a DEIB Statement** - Draft a DEIB Statement and place it at the center of your business strategy. Don't assume everyone is familiar with DEIB or shares the same viewpoint. It's important to remember that diversity, equity, and inclusion are three distinct terms that are sometimes confused or utilized in the same sentence. A DEIB statement brings all parties together. Make your DEIB statement an integral element of creating and implementing your business plan. This will enable you to make more informed decisions and hold one another accountable.

   A DEIB statement serves as a way to demonstrate commitment and a tool for the nominating committee as it considers and seeks out new board members. You should post this statement on your website, so interested potential board members can easily understand your dedication and position.

2. **Commit to Diversifying Your Board** - Representation is essential. When a prospective board member doesn't

recognize anyone who resembles them, it conveys that the organization doesn't appreciate their needs and ideas and isn't serious about DEIB. The board loses credibility with management and perhaps also with employees, clients, funders, partners, and other stakeholders if it is not both diverse and inclusive. Your board should be actively working to diversify itself. It should involve hiring for qualities that you don't currently possess but that your company will require in the future based on its path and that is typical of the populations you serve and the area in which you are located.

Review the selection criteria and recruitment objectives of your board. Start by examining the board's outwardly visible demographic composition, paying particular attention to the ethnic and gender groups that comprise a sizable portion of the workforce and are currently the most underrepresented on corporate and nonprofit boards. Additionally, broaden your applicant pool to include individuals with various cognitive perspectives, experiences, and working methods, candidates from diverse generations, personalities, and communication styles, as well as individuals from different industries and sectors. A board can significantly benefit from specific transferable skills and experiences. Your business will benefit from robust debates that result in more creative solutions to the complex problems facing the organization and its communities by forming a board that includes a broad cross-section of various perspectives and lived experiences.

3. **Adopt an equity perspective** - A board must adopt an equity mindset to recognize structural injustices and pledge to advance equity throughout the organization's

operations. A board can boost an organization's effect and contribution to the public by clearly understanding how these injustices affect the communities where the company operates and society as a whole.

To advance equity, the board must approach all its tasks with an equity mentality. This entails allocating funds, putting in place supervision to look into problems that affect disadvantaged and underrepresented groups, and ensuring that the board itself is diverse.

4. **Get Comfortable Not Feeling Comfortable** - This work is challenging, debatable, and uncomfortably uncomfortable. However, it would help if you were dedicated to the process of bringing about significant and long-lasting organizational change. You must be prepared to embrace the growing pains and challenges that come with change if you want to reap the rewards of creating a more diverse, equitable, and inclusive board for your firm's success. And to do that, one must learn to be comfortable with discomfort, which entails having difficult talks, overcoming opposition, developing new abilities, and persuading people to adopt different perspectives, attitudes, and behaviors.

5. **Take Responsibility** - A company that supports and invests in diversity, equity, and inclusion must have strong board support. The board sets the overall tone for the company; whatever it prioritizes will filter down to the rest of the company. As board members, hold each other accountable for embracing and upholding the DEIB principles, include DEIB on the agenda of board meetings frequently, include DEIB into your governance structure, and hold the CEO/president responsible for ensuring that DEIB is implemented throughout the company.

DEIB Committee or Council

Not every organization is big enough or has the budget for an official DEIB committee or council. However, that doesn't mean you can't have one. You can create a committee by recruiting from the current workforce if you are just starting out. You might be surprised by the willingness to help. Further, it is a great way to open the feedback loop and show intention and authenticity towards the DEIB effort.

If you create a committee, some ground rules will help get you up and running.

First, it is crucial to have a clear and concise understanding of the committee's purpose, roles, and responsibilities. This will help ensure everyone is on the same page and knows their job. You should be able to answer:

- Why is it being created?
- Are there specific changes you want to make or goals you want to meet?
- How does the committee fit in with the current culture?
- What are the committee's limitations?
- Who are the committee's partners?
- What roles and responsibilities will they have?
- What is the structure?

Usually, the DEIB committee conversation starts with leadership at some level. It could be the C-Suite, the Board, or even mid-level management. From there, the structure will follow. Of course, the higher up the conversation, the less red tape to get the committee up and going.

A Chief Diversity Officer might be brought in if the budget is there. Without a budget, it is possible that a C-Suite executive could carry the role in duality with an existing role. From there, other members should be added representing a cross-section of the organization.

Once the committee is formed and goals, roles, and responsibilities are laid out, you need to establish clear accountability measures. This means managing all things DEIB, following up on action items, and tracking progress. Ask:

- How will you attract or recruit members to the committee?
- How will you keep them?
- How will you evaluate what you already have and what is needed?
- How will you handle DEIB issues, concerns, discriminatory practices, or violations?
- How will you measure what is working or not working?

From there, you will want to know what initiatives you want to roll out and how. Remember, your DEIB should be 24/7/365. How will you incorporate DEIB into the daily culture? Things to consider would be:

- Communications and messages, and how they are sent. Will it be newsletters, lunch and learn, team building exercises, or creating resource groups or clubs? You need to communicate horizontally and vertically consistently.
- How will you get buy-in for budget, members, and initiatives? You need engagement.

- How will you get leadership involved consistently? Role models and superheroes will help with cultural shift, support, and enforcement.

- What mission or vision message do you want to create around your DEIB effort? If there is a theme or clear and authentic vision statement centered around belonging, engagement, and open dialog, you will see better buy-in.

The committee or council will help rally for and organize the effort. They will identify DEIB people leaders for support. So, what should the committee look for in DEIB people leaders to ensure success? Let's take a look!

People Leaders

Organizations often fail in DEIB efforts because they follow the 'dictate and direct' model from the top down. You know — the do as we say, here are the rule and consequences — no tolerance policy. We should have a circular dialog and engage leaders and influencers from every aspect of the business. Sometimes inspiration and support come from the places you least expect it. Further, you will have a better finger on the pulse of what is actually wanted, needed, and accepted.

If you don't believe me, take a survey. Talk to your LBGTQ+ community and ask them which acronym they prefer or think is accurate. I had an associate do this, and the response she received was interesting and eye-opening. The group surveyed consisted of people in the Baby Boomer and Gen X to the Gen Z crowd. The older generations preferred LGBTQ, while the younger ones insisted on LGBTQQIP2SAA or LGBTQ2S+. For this book, we decided to use LGBTQ+ for consistency and ease of recognition and reading.

There have been other surveys done regarding the term Latinx. The term became widely used on college campuses, and many now feel it is the proper term to use when addressing or discussing groups of Latin American or Caribbean ancestry. Yet, NBC News recently reported that repeated national surveys of the Hispanic/Latino communities show the term is very unpopular. The League of United Latin American Citizens (LULAC) actually dropped the use of Latinx because a poll showed that 68% of respondents preferred Hispanic and 21% preferred Latino. Only 2% described themselves as Latinx.[33]

We have had the same debates with other BIPOC. Does anyone remember the discussion on whether we should use the term African American or Black? It is still debated in some circles. What about the neurodiverse or people with disabilities? Remember the terms used not so long ago?

The point is that there is a deep and hard push for people's first language. You need to know your audience, and the best way to do that is to include them in the conversation and decision-making. It's not hard to find your DEIB people leaders. Deloitte University Press researched and found that your inclusive leaders will have six signature traits. They are:

- **Curiosity** – Curiosity equals an openness to ideas and different perspectives and tolerance for ambiguity. Inclusive leaders understand their limitations and strive for learning, creating opportunities for experiences to enable growth.

---

[33] https://www.nbcnews.com/think/opinion/many-latinos-say-latinx-offends-or-bothers-them-here-s-ncna1285916

- **Cultural Intelligence** – As noted in the examples above, they see the world differently. They often understand cultural differences and similarities and how stereotypes or mismodeling influence expectations. They value cultural differences and are adaptable to other cultural frameworks.

- **Collaborative** – Inclusive leaders are willing to collaborate, knowing they are stronger together. They are eager to share and entertain diverse perspectives knowing that empowerment and diverse perspectives lead to better innovation.

- **Commitment** – Inclusive leaders are committed to diversity because it is part of their core values and their "deep-seated sense of fairness." When a big challenge is part of the program, you need those that have the passion, energy, and drive.

- **Courage** – Inclusive leaders will speak up and call you out rather than cower and accept. They will challenge the cultural norms and will be more willing to give the feedback needed. The courageous, inclusive leader will also hold you accountable for promises.

- **Cognizance of Bias** – The are highly self-aware of unconscious bias and how it can narrow perspectives. Further, they are cognizant of process bias such as groupthink.[34]

---

[34] https://www2.deloitte.com/content/dam/Deloitte/au/Documents/human-capital/deloitte-au-hc-six-signature-traits-inclusive-leadership-020516.pdf

"Every Voice Matters"

You will find influential leaders at most levels of the organization, and you need a good cross-section when recruiting them. However, keep in mind that the higher you go, the less diverse the organization is statistically. Further, don't forget that you should consider your customer base, suppliers, regular employees, and middle management. There are people leaders hiding amongst them. If you engage them, you are better able to get buy-in from others.

You will find that each level or group may have different needs, wants, and perspectives when it comes to the DEIB framework. This could mean developing resource groups to support them and the DEIB effort as a whole.

Employee Resource Groups

Employee Resource Groups (ERG) are one of the best ways to get buy-in to the DEIB efforts you hope to initiate. It is a grassroots level of engagement with several benefits for the employees and the organization as a whole. First, it shows that you are authentic in your efforts. You show that you see your workforce, who they are, and that their perspectives matter. Further, you provide a safe (and legal) space for self-identification and engagement in the lines of communication on DEIB. ERGs round out the sense of belonging.

When you build the network through ERGs you improve employee engagement in the DEIB framework, the feedback loop, and raise cultural awareness throughout the organization. ERGs also help build connection and community through a more social link. Finally. ERGs are a more comfortable and casual way to extend leadership and learning opportunities.

If you want to consider starting ERGs, asking is the best place to start. Don't assume a particular group is needed or wanted. There are so many opportunities, but here are a few to consider:

- Interfaith or Religious ERGs
- Race, Ethnicity, Nationality ERGs
- LGBTQ+ ERG
- Working Parents or Single Parents ERG
- Social Causes and Volunteering ERG
- Professional Development ERG
- Veterans ERG
- People with Disabilities ERG
- Health and Wellness ERG
- Gaming ERG

- Also consider women, caregivers, mental health, Age-based (e.g., young professionals, seasoned professionals, intergenerational), and Region/location-based groups.

For each ERG there are a few things to consider to ensure it is successful and has the impact you want. First, you want to ensure the group has a clear purpose, structure, boundaries, etc. Second, you want the group to have leadership and management engagement, so there is a liaison between the group and the organization. Finally, consider offering group leadership incentives or formal training for group leadership.

ERGs are a great way to get buy-in and engagement from employees because they always want to know WIFM (what's in it for me). Remember that leadership support is essential no matter what type of ERGs you establish and how they are structured. Now, let's touch on that WIFM perspective for a minute.

Employee Buy-In

Change is never easy, and we naturally have a selfish streak when it comes to change at work. At work, change is primarily transactional. Employees want to know if they change or engage in change and what they will get for their effort. There is one word you can use — empowerment.

Employees get to share their stories and give input, insight, and ideas. It is their opportunity to have their voice heard and provide honest feedback on what is now and what they want or need in the future. It is about setting goals collectively and improving their sense of belonging. They also have the chance to be an ally or collaborator within a safe space, recruit new hires from their sphere, and participate in hiring, advancement or leadership, and learning opportunities.

A DEIB effort should never be about unloading more work or creating more of a burden. The organization should give more than it expects to receive. If you work from that position, you won't have to chase approval; you will attract it! And when your employees are cheerleaders, they will take the momentum to external stakeholders like customers, suppliers, potential employees, and the community.

External Stakeholders

We touched on the importance of including suppliers in the DEIB framework but now let's touch on why having external stakeholder buy-in is relevant and how we get it.

First, put on the customer hat. Think of a time you bought a product or service and were aware of the corporate culture, which made you feel good. You vowed to support that business because you wanted to support what they are doing. For example, have you ever bought a pair of TOMS shoes? They are not the most comfortable for me, but I continue to replace my TOMS because they give one-third of their profits to help make the world a better place.

Potential employees are the same way. Did you know that "34% of 18- to 34-year-olds have chosen not to apply for a job because of a lack of D&I culture in the company, whereas the percentage is 18% among those 35 to 64 years old" according to a LinkedIn survey from 2021."[35]

Customers and potential employees are part of the larger community. It isn't hard to get their buy-in or engage. All the

---

[35] https://www.linkedin.com/pulse/find-value-across-all-stakeholders-when-building-your-matias/

recent surveys and research says they are hungry for and insist on DEIB efforts. However, they are not naïve and will see through a half-hearted effort. If you want them to engage and support the effort, do as you would with your employees and make them part of the feedback loop and process. Companies survey customers all of the time for customer satisfaction. You can use the same process to match your DEIB efforts to the community as a whole! What's stopping you?

REFLECTION AND APPLICATION

- Are you part of the executive team (Board, C-Suite) that can be a superhero and advocate for the DEIB effort? If not, who is? Who are your superheroes?
- Do you have the resources for a DEIB committee or council? Who is your dream team for the committee or council based on interests, passion, and willingness?
- Who are your people leaders? Will they lead ERGs?
- Who are your external stakeholders? Can you engage them? If so, how?

CHAPTER 4

THE DEIB QUADRANT™

> *"A journey is called that because you cannot know what you will discover on the journey, what you will do, what you will find, nor what you find will do to you."*
>
> – James Baldwin

In This Chapter

- The DEIB Journey
- The Six P's
- The DEIB Quadrant: A 360° Comprehensive Approach to DEIB

About now, you might be thinking that trying to implement a strong DEIB program is above your paygrade or expertise. Or, perhaps you now realize that you want something more than implementing the traditional DEIB framework of rote memorization, videos, and multiple-choice tests annually. Hopefully, you are inspired to build a DEIB framework that breaks the 'direct and dictate' policy to create a more authentic experience built around a sense of belonging.

If that's the case, breathe. You don't have to recreate the wheel. We don't want you to do a one-off program and throw money at one-dimensional training. We have a better way to utilize a data-driven approach to build an entire ecosystem (the DEIB Lab) that will embed DEIB throughout your organization, as discussed.

The DEIB Journey

Remember, your DEIB program is not a place you get to — there is no finish line — no beginning and end. There is a beginning, but it is then a never-ending journey. I know — that sounds expensive. But it's all relative, right? I would remind you of the increased profitability and employee satisfaction that comes with a good DEIB program. It is a journey or process of continued learning, evolution, and improvement in understanding. It is a 24/7/365 effort. But once you have the proper foundation and the wheels in motion, your DEIB momentum will build, and then it is all about maintenance! It is Newton's law — an object in motion will stay in motion.

For now, let's focus on the beginning with the journey in mind. Every journey begins with a purpose — the 'why' are we doing this. There has to be a purpose or meaning that resonates.

By now, in our personal lives, we have all heard or been told to find your 'why' — find your purpose, the meaning. We have done mental acrobats to figure out what gives us personal meaning. If you have, you are now practiced in that exercise. You can take that and apply it to your DEIB effort. Finding the reason for your effort is the first step in the journey, and it begins with a conversation.

Why do you want a DEIB program? Are you looking to be a better corporate citizen in the world? Does your reason stem from personal experiences? What are your desired outcomes of a successfully implemented effort? And what is the need?

Consider your organizational values, beliefs, and culture if you need a nudge. What are they?

Ask Questions

There is no better place to begin connecting values or exposing gaps that by asking questions. Take those values and beliefs and then add sentences like:

- I feel like I do (or don't) BELONG because (fill in the blank).
- I feel like I am (or am not) HEARD because (fill in the blank).

Do they align? For example, does the organization say and believe employees come first? How are the two questions answered? Would you say you don't feel like you belong because you suffer a guilt trip every time you need to call in because your child is sick? Or would you say you belong because management understands when you have to call in? Maybe you have a shared shift program to help those parents. It is crazy how subtle it can sometimes be, right?

So often, organizations will have a mission or value system that they think aligns, but it doesn't. You have to be ready to embed DEIB in your values. Here's another example. Your organization says they value employee feedback. Yet, when an employee goes to a manager to point out a serious violation, the manager tells the employee to keep their head down and not cause any waves. Nobody wants to lose their job, right?

Ask questions and take surveys about stated values and perceived values. What is said compared to the action taken?

It would help if you embedded your DEIB in your values. So, if your value statement currently says your employees matter, they come first (or some version of that), change it to say something like, 'we value and SUPPORT the DIVERSITY' of our employees. If you believe everyone should and you want everyone to have a sense of belonging, say it! But whatever you do, take time to really connect your purpose — your WHY to it.

The objective is to build an inclusive culture and a sense of belonging. You want everyone internally and externally to list all the reasons they feel connected to the organization — not all the ways they don't.

The Sliding Scale and Courage

Now, with every journey we take, some will travel at a faster or slower pace. Some will have a better understanding of the terrain while others struggle. Then some are on the journey because they didn't have a choice (teenagers on the family outing, anyone?). Understanding that everyone will have different comfort levels, knowledge, and even willingness to participate is crucial. This means you have to consider meeting everyone at their tempo. You will have those that are deeply passionate because it is personal. Then you will have those who, no matter what you do to encourage them, will fight against every effort to get on board.

The trick is to approach everyone like a mentor and coach. Offer safe spaces to work through uncomfortable conversations. You have to be open to dialogue without condemnation or judgment on both sides. It would be best if you worked from the position that those with strong views often have a personal attachment. You are the bridge over troubled waters.

Without going into all the politics and polarization, suffice it to say that there is noise — and it is loud. You may feel it is an impossible task. However, if you create an environment where each side doesn't feel like they are being coerced or pressured to agree or disagree, you will begin to open a path forward. It is about building trust and understanding that everyone has different world views, identities, and experiences. It is complex. The goal is only to share those different perspectives and work to understand other people's points of view.

Start by Addressing the Status Quo for Common Ground

It is no longer okay to live and work by the status quo. And I would argue that if you talked to each side of the spectrum — those passionate for DEIB and those entirely against it — they each have a status quo perspective, and both need improvement or updating. I challenge you to ask both sides what they think diversity is. Most of the polarization stems from diversity being a Black and white issue (sometimes LGBTQ+). It used to be a woman versus man issue.

Diversity is an ever-evolving conversation. How does either side feel about Boomers or Millennials? How do they feel about grandpa still having a driver's license? What about working next to the homeless person? What if that homeless person was a single mom who escaped domestic violence? What about that really annoying guy that thinks he knows everything? He is a person with autism and doesn't know how to have a social conversation; this is his first job.

You see, when you take the hyped media out of the equation, you can begin to have honest conversations about how complex diversity is. It starts from a position of kindness. Instead of starting from the typical perspective of 'us against them,' find a way to show humility and the assumptions we often make. Encourage everyone to share how they are different if they want to. Again, it is not about the 'direct and dictate' but about opening the door to conversation.

Working through these steps is key to developing a DEIB program that has staying power and will be unique to your organization. Remember, authenticity is one of the missing links between a good and failed DEIB effort. You can't put forth a program that doesn't speak to the wants and needs of your organizational ecosystem.

The iSuccess DEIB framework does precisely that. So, while I want to introduce you to the process, keep in mind that this is an introduction in broad brush strokes. If you feel something is not addressed, it is purely because it most likely lives in the details specific to your organization.

The Six Ps and the DEIB Quadrant

The Six Ps and DEIB Quadrant are two components of the proprietary framework we use to create a best-in-class DEIB initiative for your organization. The Six Ps are Perspective, People, Processes, Positioning, Precision, and Passion. Two of the six P's (Precision and Passion) are the organization's sole responsibility.

The other four make up the DEIB Quadrant, where we work with our clients to help create a program unique to the organizational needs.

Together, all six are the house in which your program lives. Here is what we mean:

1. **Passion** – is the organizational commitment and dedication to the program. It is the ground you build your program on. If the ground is unstable, the house cannot stand. Passion is one of the two Ps that is the organization's sole responsibility. If you don't have the passion, you must create, build, and maintain it, so everything else is stable.

2. **Precision** – is the second P solely in the organization's hands. It is the cap or roof of your DEIB program. Precision is the feedback loop you create with ongoing assessments utilizing organization-specific metrics to measure the success of each process in your program. Without this cap piece, everything under it is susceptible to the elements and storms that can ravage what you built. The roof holds the house in place and protects it from storms.

3. **Perspective** – is one-half of the foundation you build everything else on. It includes personal and business perspectives. Perspective is the mindset, beliefs, and thoughts that we must shift to lead to changed behaviors. Unless there is a shift in perspective, it will be business as usual. On one front, we present the business case for DEIB to help leaders shift their perspective to understand that DEIB is part of the business strategy. It helps give their company a competitive edge. We challenge their past beliefs and assumptions. Finally, we help them acknowledge that the

process will be an ongoing journey, not a one-time event. On the second front, we gather a true **perspective** of what leaders and employees think. We listen to internal and external stakeholders' feedback about diversity, equity, inclusion, and belonging through a multitude of conversations. This includes one-on-one interviews, focus groups, and anonymous surveys. We challenge them to recognize their own unconscious or implicit bias (perspective), which directly affects how they approach DEIB.

4. **People** – are the other half of the DEIB foundation. This is where we create alignment at all levels. Your people include the Board, C-Suite, DEIB committee, people leaders, managers, employees, internal and external stakeholders, and your suppliers or external vendors.

5. **Processes** – will be how we design a program. It consists of a DEIB policy and commitment statement, recruiting, interviewing, and screening processes. It also includes hiring, onboarding, compensation, and pay equity practices or processes. We work through workplace policies like equitable promotion and advancement processes, internal and external communications about DEIB policies, and a supplier diversity process. When building a house, you have different components selected and unique to how you want to live, like your appliances, flooring, cabinets, and even the lights and fixtures you choose. Processes are like this piece of your DEIB house.

6. **Positioning** – is the visible support and commitment to DEIB organization-wide. If you keep with the house theme, this is the paint color, furniture, and décor you choose to create and reinforce DEIB within your culture. It is about creating a culture of inclusivity and belonging.

You want people to come in, feel relaxed, and sink into that cozy sofa, right? It starts with leadership leading a strategy, people leaders and managers reinforcing the strategy, and employees living the strategy.

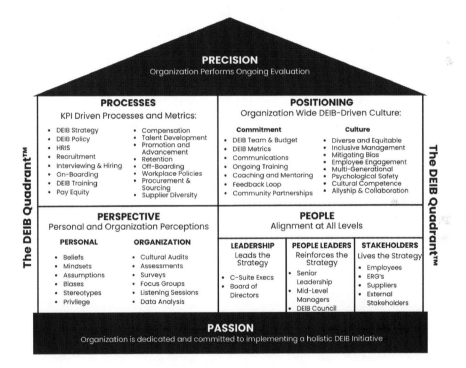

When you put all the pieces together, this is what it looks like from ground to sky. The six Ps and the DEIB Quadrant help build the house you want to live in. And every home, no matter how new, requires ongoing maintenance like everything else—our bodies, cars, relationships. So, it isn't about building it and forgetting it. If you do that, it will deteriorate and eventually lose its value!

REFLECTION AND APPLICATION

Look at your DEIB house:

- Is the ground your DEIB house is built on solid, is the passion there? If not, why?
- Do you have a strong foundation in your people and perspectives? Both are the supports to everything that comes after.
- What do your positioning and processes look like? Is your DEIB house built to be inviting and give a sense of belonging?
- Finally, is the roof leaky? Do you have an adequate feedback loop?

CHAPTER 5

TWO SIDES OF THE DEIB STORY

> *"Creating and managing a diverse workforce is a process, not a destination."*
> – R. Roosevelt Thomas, Jr.

In This Chapter

- The Diversity Audit
- Performing a DEIB Audit
- Analyzing the Data to Create a DEIB Strategy
- Reflection and Application

The DEIB audit assesses the degree of diversity within the organization at all levels. It considers pay equity, human resource policies, diversity of the supplier base, and other diversity-related factors.[36]

The purpose is to assess programs, policies, procedures, and practices critically and honestly across the organization regarding diversity, equity, and inclusion to strengthen your DEIB strategic approach. Further, the assessment allows us to conduct an organizational gap analysis to understand the current baseline and identify areas of change. In this phase, community data, internal data, and their respective trends are all important. The audit also ensures you get the right people helping you, folks good with slicing and dicing data in meaningful ways. The caveat is to do the audit and not fall victim to analysis paralysis while still diving deep enough to prompt meaningful insight to action.

The benefits of doing a DEIB audit are vast but let's focus on two with high impact. First, the audit can spur innovation and creativity when laying out your DEIB strategy. For example, did you know that according to a recent HR survey, 91% of the workforce believes that companies should offer personalized benefits packages, and one of the most desired benefits is pet insurance?[37] When talking about generational gaps, the same survey reveals that Boomers are more concerned with health care, while Gen X is concerned about financial security and student loan debt. The point is that an audit can expose your weak spots in policies and benefits and bring to light solutions that people want and will get on board with. If offering pet insurance and student loan assistance isn't new and innovative, what is?!

Second, a DEIB audit is probably one of the most powerful statements you can make about your commitment to DEIB.

---

[36] https://internalaudit360.com/is-it-time-to-conduct-a-diversity-and-inclusion-audit/

[37] https://www.amwins.com/resources-insights/article/the-bottom-line-of-benefits-for-a-5-generation-workforce

When your employees see you are taking actionable and visible steps to increase diversity, it sends a loud message that you care and are dedicated to making it happen. You will eventually improve employee retention and attract top talent that values a diverse work culture.

Performing the DEIB Audit

We perform an audit by gathering a true perspective of what leaders and employees think by conducting surveys through the organization. It is best to do anonymous surveys to get honest feedback and build trust for the DEIB process. Another great way to work through the feedback and gain trust is through focus groups. We help get focus groups set up and give guidance or monitor the process so attention remains on the goals of the DEIB effort. At the same time, we audit any current DEIB efforts and data. For example, do you have data on how many BIPOC, women, veterans, employees with disabilities, or LGBTQ+ employees you have? Do you know the average age of your employees or their socio-economic background? Do you have any formal or informal ERGs? What do your job descriptions look like? Hiring practices? Discrimination policies and procedures?

The assessment process is about digging through the weeds and closets to find what is there or isn't there. It is a deep dive and taking inventory. We talk about the journey.

Think about when you are packing for an extended vacation or camping trip. You dig the suitcase out. Maybe there are old baggage tags left from the last trip. Maybe you have to dig out the tent and the cooler. You clean them up. Remove the old tags. Maybe you notice the tent has a hole in it, or the drain plug is missing on the cooler. The handle or wheel is broken on the suitcase. So, you have to repair and replace before you can pack.

You get to the store and realize your suitcase or tent doesn't fit your current needs. So, you begin assessing what you need now. Does it need to be bigger or smaller? How often will it get used? Is there a better option or new technology since you used the last one?

Your DEIB audit is the same way. What you thought was fine and did the job may no longer work. Maybe you need to expand for a more extended staying power. Perhaps you see where improvements have been made, and you need to upgrade. You do the assessment not only to flush out the bad but also to find what will serve your DEIB efforts, what won't, and what needs to be repaired, replaced, or added.

Best Survey Questions for a DEIB Audit

Whether you do anonymous surveys, focus groups, or some other method to gather data, there are some fundamental questions you can ask to get the conversations started. They include:

- Do you feel there is enough diversity in the executive team?

- Do you feel the evaluation and promotion process is free from bias?

- Do you feel we encourage and celebrate diverse people and ideas?

- Do you feel we work to attract diverse talent and talent from underrepresented communities?

- Do you feel comfortable talking about your social or cultural background at work?
- Do you feel the needs of coworkers with disabilities are adequately supported?
- Do you feel you can communicate concerns freely and without fear?

The key is to ask questions that encourage perspective. Asking 'do you feel' questions will hit on whether there is a sense of belonging. No matter if you think you are doing something right, it is all about perspective and how it is received or viewed by recipients.

There are also industry or organization-specific questions you may want to ask. This is a general list to get started. You will analyze the data from there to find themes, gaps, or even what you are doing right!

Analyzing the Data

As mentioned, you don't want to get stuck in the data and fear making the wrong decision. Remember, this is a DEIB journey. Not everything will have a perfect ten landing on the first run. The key is analyzing the data to create a strategy using broad brush strokes. Don't get lost in the weeds. For example, earlier, we covered the proper use of the LGBTQ+ acronym or the switch from Latino to Latinx and back again. You can't please everyone all the time.

What we mean by broad brush strokes is to say that you have every intention to make the best effort to use people-first language (PFL). People first language works to prioritize the personhood of an individual instead of their identity or diagnosis. The phrase initial stems from communicating in a way that reflects respect for the person and doesn't describe someone based on their disability. It can extend to reflect how we describe groups of people. For example, when talking about 'slaves,' it is now more accurate to describe this group of people as 'enslaved persons.' We shift focus on the person and not what was thrust upon them. Another example is changing from an 'epileptic person' or autistic person to a 'person with epilepsy or a 'person with autism.'

Do you see the broad strokes? PFL is the broad stroke in your DEIB effort.

From there, it is about authenticity. For example, at the beginning of the book, there is mention that we chose to use LGBTQ+ for ease of reading, the acronym frequently changing to include other groups, and the global recognition of the acronym. It isn't about the exclusion of any particular section of that group. We are writing a book on diversity, so hopefully, it is clear that our authenticity gives license to the choice we make.

The same goes for your organization. If you are authentic, analyze the data, and it shows that a large population of your workforce prefers Latinx, then you may decide to use that rather than Latino. Or maybe you use broad brush strokes and use BIPOC.

The bottom line is that the data will guide you in creating your strategy. The key is to use the data to take those first steps. If you can't run, you walk. If you can't walk, you crawl. Remember that it is about positive forward movement!

REFLECTION AND APPLICATION

- Consider if the organization has ever completed a thorough DEIB audit.
- If you completed a previous DEIB audit, what was learned?
- Have you made improvements, or did you end up with analysis paralysis?
- If you have never completed a DEIB audit, why?

CHAPTER 6

DEVELOPING YOUR DEIB ROADMAP

> *"All you need is the plan, the roadmap, and the courage to press on to your destination."*
> ~ Earl Nightingale

In This Chapter

- Preparation (Steps 1-3)
- Development (Steps 4-6)
- Implementation (Steps 7-9)
- Review and Refine (10-12)
- Reflection and Application

Have you ever gotten in the car and drove without a destination? If so, my guess is it is infrequent. Deep down, even if we think we will drive aimlessly, we usually have a destination we are automatically drawn to. You typically have a route in mind even when you decide on a Sunday to take a scenic drive. Building your DEIB strategy is the same way. You don't take off and start driving without a general destination in mind. Yes, your DEIB journey is just that—a journey. However, you don't want to get lost in the wilderness. You never know what's out there lurking about!

With that, we visited the DEIB audit and how to perform one. That is the first step in building a strategy. After all, you need to know where you are and where you want to go. You also need to understand how you are going to get there. Will it be by train, plane, or automobile?

Preparation

Whenever we take a journey, we have to prepare. We take inventory and assess what we have or what we will need. We make lists; we discuss itineraries; we may add or drop plans based on some democratic process. This is no different. The roadmap to the DEIB journey starts with preparation.

Step 1 – Establish the Baseline. The key is to build a data-driven strategy. The DEIB audit will shed light on what people think is working and what isn't. However, you might not get all the data you need from surveys or focus groups. For example, you may not obtain specific demographic information on age, gender, sexual orientation, or other sensitive data. It is a fine line to walk when trying to protect people's rights and privacy and learn what you need to increase your diversity effort. For that reason, you may need to track data location demographics or other outside sources.

Another consideration would be to do a trends and intersectionality analysis. A trends analysis focused on historic employment patterns like hiring, pay raises, etc. In comparison, an intersectionality analysis will look for patterns where those that cross two or more diversity groups have experienced difficulties in the workplace. For example, Black women cross two underrepresented groups. Analyzing intersectionality can bring to light other trends you may not have seen otherwise.

No matter where you start, the DEIB strategy needs to be based on the data so you aren't driving around aimlessly, wasting time, and getting lost. So, where do you start once you have the data and see the trends, gaps, or what is working?

The data you gather and analyze will establish your baseline.

Step 2 – Secure Commitment to Drive Change. Once you have the baseline and can report the trends or gaps, it is essential to garner the attention of those who can act and are on board to drive change. This process includes working from the Board and C-Suite all the way down to the employees and suppliers.

Step 3 – Establish a DEIB Council. Once you have gained buy-in vertically and horizontally, you will have a clearer vision of your DEIB leaders. When you do, you want to work with them to establish your DEIB council or committee for governance and accountability.

Development

If we stick with the travel analogy, we usually see people step up and take on specific roles. You will have someone who will offer to drive the rental car or scope out the hotel lounge. One person is ready to research activities or navigate to local tourist spots. Then some are along for the ride but need to be told what to do because they aren't sure what they have to offer. This is how the development of your DEIB strategy will play out. You will have your enthusiastic adventure ready to be the tour guide and those that want to go on the trip but need help getting from place to place.

Step 4 – Create a DEIB Strategic Plan. This is where cross-functional teams and the council or committee will develop goals or objectives and then monitor the progress of the DEIB effort. They will determine the metrics or KPIs to use and then ensure the feedback loop operates efficiently.

Step 5 – Develop Employee Resource Groups (ERGs). The committee or council will work to help set up and support Employee Resource Groups. The goal is to place people leaders within the groups and encourage participation through peer support. The ERGs will be a vital resource to the committee and strengthen the feedback and assessment process, and leadership support and engagement here are crucial.

Step 6 – Establish a DEIB Policy. Once the committee and ERGs have worked to determine what is considered vital to the organizational ecosystem, you can establish a DEIB policy and statement. This is where the organization will memorialize its commitment to DEIB by explaining how they see DEIB connecting to the company's mission and give examples of DEIB efforts or initiatives the company will undertake.

Implementation

This is where the rubber really meets the road, so to speak. Until now, you have planned, organized, discussed, put ideas on paper, and strategized. Now, it is time to put your money where your mouth it. This is where you have to walk the walk and show your commitment—and it will show—action or no action. You are now on center stage. If you have adequately prepared and developed your strategy, you should have a good idea of where you are going. If not, you will be the one who refuses to ask for directions when lost (does anyone have a travel partner like that—or are you that person?).

Step 7 – Recruit and Hire Diverse Talent. By now, I think HR, managers, recruiters, and even the C-Suite knows we need to recruit and hire diverse talent. However, there is a disconnect where these groups say they try but can't find enough qualified candidates from diverse groups. The issue is that your methods are flawed, and you aren't looking in the right places. Further, your culture hasn't been one that creates a vision of belonging. Too harsh? Let's call it tough love!

You have to meet diverse people where they are, not where you want them to be or think they are. If you are looking for young recruits or talent right out of high school, are you talking to school counselors who are coaching gifted students, or are you going to the local youth group, Boys and Girls Club, or YMCA? Further, are you using exclusive language in your job postings or descriptions? It is always a good idea to clean the house, and a deep clean is needed every so often, no matter how squeaky clean you think the place is.

Step 8 – Inclusive Performance Management. Your inclusive performance management system will be the feedback loop to ensure you stay accountable to your DEIB objectives. Typically, there are three types of traditional performance management systems. There is the balanced scorecard, management by objectives, and budget-driven business plans.[38] No matter which system you use, the key is to address any biases in the system. For DEIB-specific performance management, you may want to consider DEIB-specific software as it works to remove bias.

Step 9 – Equitable and Inclusive Culture. Let's say it again; it starts at the top. Leadership will be the role model for building an equitable and inclusive culture. From there, no matter who is on the team or part of the ecosystem, you then need to hire and support people who are open to working with others who are different from themselves. Open-mindedness and self-awareness of bias are key. Building an equitable and inclusive culture requires humility and willingness to challenge the status quo and be open to being challenged.

---

[38] https://www.clearpointstrategy.com/types-of-performance-management-systems/

Review and Refine

This is a journey—there is a beginning but never an end. We live in a world that is constantly changing and evolving. Think back to the history and the timeline of DEIB. We have traveled a long distance. Yet, there is so much more to do. What we know to be acceptable now will change and expand or morph. The whole idea behind DEIB is about being open-minded and receptive to better understanding and different perspectives. Thus, there must be steps on the roadmap that allow for a constant feedback loop and opportunity for growth.

Step 10 - Communications (Internal and External) - Your DEIB Journey. Communication is a wonderful thing—when done correctly. Therefore, you should consider a DEIB communications strategy. Deloitte recently shared that you should focus on four things when considering your communications strategy. Your strategy should be branded, intentional, engaging, and holistic.[39] This means your communications should be planned and on purpose, consistent, and authentic. Further, the communication should invite dialogue—the give and take of sharing information and listening. Finally, there should be a personal story or message. Humility around our own bias, asking questions without making assumptions, and listening to others' stories bring the richness needed to any DEIB effort. You then extend this strategy outward and share the message of your journey with the external stakeholders.

Step 11 - Focus on Marketplace and Community Impact. When you give attention to the external ecosystem—that of your

---

[39] https://www2.deloitte.com/us/en/blog/human-capital-blog/2022/dei-communication-strategy.html

marketplace, the communities in which you conduct business, you strengthen your DEIB effort. Outreach is a beautiful thing, it's like adding fuel to the fire of your DEIB efforts. It's about recognizing that your organization doesn't exist in a vacuum – it's part of a larger ecosystem, and what happens in that ecosystem can have a big impact on your ability to foster diversity, equity, inclusion, and belonging.

So, why does focusing on the marketplace and community matter so much? Well, for starters, it opens up a whole world of diverse recruiting opportunities. By actively engaging with different communities and demographics, you can tap into talent pools that you may not have even known existed. And let me tell you, diversity in your workforce isn't just a nice-to-have – it's a game-changer. It brings fresh perspectives, new ideas, and innovative thinking to the table, which can be a huge competitive advantage in today's fast-paced diverse world.

But it's not just about recruiting – it's also about enhancing your brand reputation and connecting with your customers on a deeper level. When you show that you care about diversity, equity, inclusion, and belonging in your marketplace and community, it sends a powerful message about your organization's values. People want to do business with companies that align with their own beliefs and values, and by demonstrating your commitment to DEIB, you can build trust and loyalty with your customers.

And let's not forget about the social impact side of things. Engaging with your marketplace and community in DEIB efforts isn't just good for business – it's good for society as a whole. By giving back and supporting initiatives that promote diversity and inclusion, you're not only making a positive difference in people's lives, but you're also contributing to a more equitable and just world. And that's something worth striving for, don't you think?

So, as you move forward with your DEIB journey, remember to keep an eye on the world outside your organization. Because when you focus on your marketplace and community impact, you're not just making your organization better – you're making the world a better place too.

Step 12 – Embed Supplier Diversity into Procurement. This is where you focus on trade groups and nonprofits that support minority-owned businesses and suppliers. Further, focus on your current suppliers and get to know them. Does someone from a historically marginalized group own them? If so, they could be your next DEIB advocate and introduce you to other supplies in their network. You can then build a more diverse supplier network, help advance their business, and support those communities. It only takes a spark to ignite a fire! And when you embed supplier diversity into your procurement, you create a synergistic ecosystem that provides procurement opportunities to these suppliers. This give and take—ebb and flow—helps suppliers grow and allows your organization to help them develop and scale where everyone can become more efficient and profitable. From there, your supplier relationship will extend to improving the local economy and communities in which you and they are located.

Putting the Pieces Together

By now, you may have gathered that it is a habit to weave a story into the process. Doing so helps visualize the possibilities. So, bear with me and see how all the moving pieces can fall into place and create a beautifully organic DEIB story for an organization.

I learned of this story of extraordinary DEIB execution in the insurance industry through an acquaintance. A particular agency owner spoke to my acquaintance about how he found his niche market. Little did he know that his focus and passion for DEIB was what set him apart and helped build his empire.

Like anyone, he started in the business as a generalist. However, being in the military and traveling, he was passionate about diverse cultures. He wanted to find a way to differentiate his business while incorporating his passion for rich culture. His focus wasn't necessarily on DEIB in the most structured sense. The focus was on integrating his joy of different cultures into his business strategy. So, he set out and did some research. This research led him to the reality that a large majority of businesses in the area were owned primarily by people of Asian descent. The spectrum was broad and included everything from wholesalers and dry cleaners to restaurants.

Frankly, he felt surprised that he hadn't noticed before, but that quickly turned to a sense of being overwhelmed. He wasn't sure where to start, but he needed to start. He decided to eat the elephant one bite at a time. He took the first step and focused on the dry cleaning business. He then developed a plan of action. It was a four-pronged approach focused on understanding culture and customs.

The Audit

He began by doing an audit of what he designated as Asian-owned businesses. He found that insurance standards severely underrepresented this population of businesses. Their policies and services were adequate at best. Further, he was surprised by the lack of cultural sensitivity and language barrier within the insurance industry related to this group.

He dug in and studied his business and the needs of this group in detail.

The Commitment

Once he determined his baseline, he focused on his organizational commitment. The first thing he recognized is he couldn't go all in and support this sector of business without having someone who could help him communicate. So, he hired not one but two bilingual associates. He needed two, so if one was off, there was a backup, and his clients always had their needs met. This would be the start of his DEIB committee.

Developing Strategy

Once he had a few associates on board, he shifted focus on working to understand the culture, customs, and needs of the community—not only the business owners but their suppliers and customers. He is humble when he shares that, at first, he didn't understand the nuance of the cultures within the culture.

For example, he expressed how he had always brought a woman interpreter to meetings with his clients who were Korean or Chinese. Those clients saw the gesture as one to build trust. Yet, the client was offended when he brought the interpreter to a meeting with a Hindi client. This client felt they spoke English well and didn't need an interpreter.

This lesson of cultures within cultures continued to play out. He realized that he could find distinct cultures outside of personal identities. Distinct cultures exist in different industries. For example, there is a specific culture in the construction or real estate industry—just as there is a culture within each individual organization.

The point is that he learned to be empathetic and authentic while communicating he was attempting to make his best effort to serve the group's needs.

Implementing and Executing

As the business owner, he continued to evaluate his bias, his process, and what worked or didn't. Once he had a foot in the market, his focus shifted within his organizational ecosystem to improve the inclusivity of his business. He focused on recruiting and hiring associates from the community he wanted to serve. There was a new concentration on understanding the specific specialties. He looked at coverage requirements for these business owners. Much of which had been neglected by others up to this point.

Refinement

It was about communicating consistently and building an authentic or genuine connection to the community. He would ask questions about these business owners' pain points or blind spots, how his business could offer better services, or what was missing. He created partnerships built on trust.

His strong connections eventually led to an expanded focus on other Asian-owned businesses. The network effortlessly flowed from dry cleaning to Chinese and Korean restaurants. From there, he was introduced to meat suppliers, packaging wholesalers, and even accountants and sign makers. His agency became the go-to insurance agency in that community. His clients knew he was sincere. However, they also knew he took the time to become knowledgeable in all the intricacies and cross-business issues his clients dealt with. His depth of knowledge expanded from his profession to the culture.

This is a perfect example of precision in DEIB efforts.

REFLECTION AND APPLICATION

Ironically, the twelve steps resemble the proverbial twelve-step rehabilitation program. While there is (or was) no intention for similarities, it is oddly familiar to think of building the road map based on rehabilitation. With that, think about the following:

- Do I have everything I need to create a baseline to start from?
- Are we secure in having a commitment and confidence in who will chair a DEIB committee?
- What do we want DEIB policies and strategies to focus on?
- Do we have or are we ready to establish ERGs?
- What is the plan for recruiting, hiring, and performance management?
- What can we do to improve our culture to be more inclusive?
- What is our communications strategy?
- Have we developed a plan for review and refinement?

CHAPTER 7

NOT ALL TRAINING IS CREATED EQUAL

> *"Tell me and I forget, teach me and I may remember, involve me and I learn."*
> ~ Benjamin Franklin

In This Chapter

- Why Most DEIB Training Fails
- Experiential Learning
- Measuring the Impact of DEIB Training
- Comprehensive and Ongoing Training for Success
- Reflection and Application

There is training, and then there is TRAINING. What does that mean?

Unfortunately, most DEIB training has historically focused on bringing awareness. In the beginning, maybe that is what we needed—or thought we needed. However, we have now been through awareness training for decades. It is a safe bet to say we are all well versed in awareness. I mean, when is the last time you went to a DEIB training video or presentation and said, "oh, wow—I wasn't aware of THAT." If you have, let's chat! I would love to hear what new information is out there and why you weren't aware.

DEIB Training Failures

It's been said before and a few times throughout this book. The biggest issue with DEIB training is that the training is usually some one-off event that speaks at you and isn't consistently reinforced or embedded into the organizational DNA. Again, the training is some video dusted off once a year and thrown into the VCR in a conference room.

Okay— maybe I exaggerate because you ask what a VCR is, but you get the point. The execution is old and outdated and not based on what works.

Another failure of typical DEIB training is that there is no emotional attachment, and the training is not tied to an overall DEIB strategy aligned with the business strategy. We are human and can't help but ask **what's in it for me**. It is hard for us to change behavior or create new habits if we don't see the benefit and can attach to it in a personal way.

If you don't believe me, consider the argument author, James Clear, makes in *Atomic Habits*. He says there are four laws of behavior change. For change to happen or to create new habits, the change or habit should be made obvious, attractive, easy, and satisfying.[40] He will say that if one variable is missing, then change will not happen. Now you may think he is just another *guru* trying to sell books. In that case, let's explore the science behind behavioral change. It starts with the brain.

Training and the Brain

Our brain is a network of pathways built on stories and experiences throughout our lives. When we are babies, our brain is like a blank slate. For every story or experience, we create neural pathways. For example, we touch something hot, and that experience creates a neural message sending a signal that when you touch something hot, it hurts. Do it enough times, and we stop touching hot things.

Now, some pathways continue to get used repeatedly, so our reactions or interactions are almost automatic. Think of the child athlete or musician who practices and becomes a professional. The skills and abilities are practically instinctual at some point. Think about driving to work every day. Do you recall times when you can't remember if you stopped at a stop sign because driving was almost automatic? The brain has built a super-highway for these activities.

Conversely, think of when you were in school and forced to take physical education or music class. You couldn't wait to be done. Your brain is introduced to a particular activity and forced to repeat it. By the end of the semester or year, you are better, but five years down the road, you cannot remember what you learned. This is because the brain prunes the neural pathways or connections we don't use.

---

[40] Clear, James. 2018. Atomic Habits: Tiny Changes, Remarkable Results: An Easy & Proven Way to Build Good Habits & Break Bad Ones. New York, New York: Avery, an imprint of Penguin Random House.

Let's look at it from another perspective. Have you ever been to a large college or business campus where sidewalks lead from one building to the others? Most often, grassy knolls or gardens break up the ridged look and feel of the concrete paths. The hustle and bustle on the sidewalks consist of the hurried pace of people trying to get from one destination to the other.

On occasion, you will see a worn path in the grass where now and then, someone ignores the *stay off the grass* sign and risks the schedule of sprinklers coming on to get to some other area less traveled. Initially, the path starts with someone walking through the grass. Eventually, observers see that others have taken this route and decide to venture across. One leads to ten, to one hundred. Over a period of time, the grass is worn away, the dirt begins to show, and the path widens. Sometimes, the dirt path is eventually paved.

This is how our brain and neural pathways work. The messages or people will usually take the concrete sidewalk because it is the path of least resistance. There is less risk of getting wet, muddy or yelled at for being on the grass. However, at some point, the story changes, and the benefit outweigh the risk, so we venture in a new direction.

So, what's the point of this long-winded explanation of how the brain works?

First, it clarifies how it is hard to break thinking patterns or habits in how we do things. Second, the examples bring to light the necessity for experiential learning.

Experiential Learning

DEIB training often fails because the training is detached from how we learn. It doesn't have the sticking power. To be successful, DEIB training needs to incorporate experiential learning.

So, what is experiential learning, and how do we incorporate experiential learning best practices into our DEIB training strategy?

Let's start with what it is. Experiential learning is a process where people learn from their own experiences and observations. Simply, we learn best by doing and reflecting on the activities or tasks. This type of learning stands in contrast to didactic learning, which relies primarily on listening to lectures or reading texts.

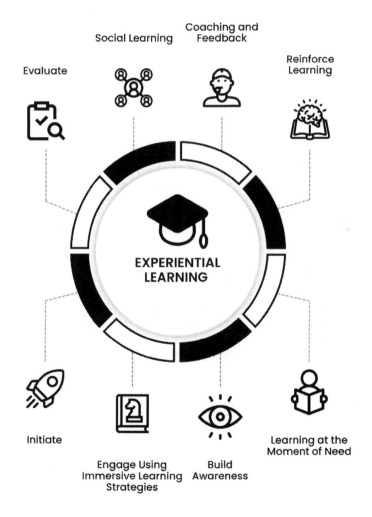

Experiential learning begins with initiating and engaging immersive learning strategies. The immersive activities are meant to bring forward awareness but then build on the learning needs at that moment. In this way, experiential learning is more organic and adaptive to the variables within that time and place. Then, the knowledge is reinforced through doing. Perhaps it is labs, experiments, role-playing, or some other hands-on exercise. While reinforcement learning takes place, there is a feedback loop and coaching or mentorship—eventually, the learning shifts to a social learning context followed by evaluation.

The medical, legal and even skilled trades go through experiential learning. After all, you don't want a doctor to finish reading a few books, watching some videos, and then do brain surgery. Further, you may not want someone working on your car or electrical without knowing they have experience. Well, experience comes by doing—doing under supervision at first.

In the DEIB world, one way to incorporate experiential learning into DEIB training is by using simulations and role-playing exercises. Simulations allow participants to apply what they've learned in a safe environment. Role-playing exercises help participants to understand how they might react in real-world situations.

When designing experiential learning activities, it's essential to keep the following principles in mind:

- **Active participation:** Participants should be actively involved in the activity, not just observing.

- **Reflection:** Participants should have time to reflect on their experiences and what they've learned.

- **Real-world relevance:** The activity should be relevant to the real world and the participants' work environment.

- **Safety:** Participants should feel safe to experiment and make mistakes without fear of negative consequences.

When used effectively, experiential learning activities can be a powerful tool for DEIB training.

Experiential Learning Best Practices

Younger generations are very familiar with experiential learning. Yet, it doesn't mean that their experiences were positive. Have you ever tried to do role play training? The moans and grumbles are almost automatic, deafening, and definitely unapologetic! Not everyone is an actor or wants to be put on stage. Further, the one person who does—well, that is the instigator or the one who likes to play devil's advocate to the extreme purposefully. So, before you automatically decide to create role-play activities, read the room and consider the following best practices:

1. Develop **common ground** based on finding similar priorities, values, and goals to help align colleagues and get everyone on the same path forward. Consider an initial survey to start the conversation.

2. Encourage **facilitated conversation training** that creates an open space for ALL employees (including fewer vocal ones) to be heard, issues to be brought up, concerns voiced, and feedback given.

3. Incorporate **cultural sensitivity** into training to help dominant group members understand how to better empathize with colleagues of under-represented cultures, backgrounds, or identities.

4. Train on Unconscious Bias to **uncover and identify** the subconscious ways in which we engage in biased or oppressive behaviors and practices.

5. Empower diverse employees to advocate for how they can be better accommodated in the workplace.

6. Allow employees with different physical, environmental, or religious needs to drive the creation of spaces in which they feel comfortable and safe.

7. Train managers on inclusive management to help supervisors recognize discriminatory or oppressive management practices and dismantle biased systems within the workplace.

8. Train on **community engagement** which goes beyond your internal organization and encourages team members to look at how your business can serve the greater community through the lens of DEIB.

9. Build capabilities that positively impact behavior change.

10. Teach employees how to go from ally to collaborator and actively support and uplift their marginalized colleagues.

11. Offer a broad range of training covering subjects such as anti-racism, anti-sexism, anti-transphobia, and more.

Now, here's the thing—you don't have to try everything at once. Remember, it is a journey. You have a roadmap. When we travel or take a vacation, excursions and activities are planned out based on where we are at the moment. Further, if you mix too many activities at once, it can be hard to measure success. We want time to measure the impact of whatever training we implement.

Measuring The Impact of Training

So, how do you measure the impact of training? It can sometimes be like trying to nail Jell-O to the wall. However, you will begin to see signs. Here are some things to look for:

- **Leadership** – Are you beginning to see diverse representation in management at all levels of leadership, including the C-suite and board of directors? If not, have you been training diverse people for those positions? Are you mentoring and coaching internally to elevate from within?

- **Retention** – Are you finding turnover has slowed? Do employees enjoy their jobs and feel they have equal access to opportunities for advancement and upskilling? Do they feel they belong?

- **Program Engagement** - Are your workforce education, mentorship, and other continuous learning programs used? Has engagement increased since you implemented DEIB training?

- **Employee Feedback** - How does your workforce feel about the company culture regarding DEIB? Do they feel served by DEIB initiatives? Do they think current DEIB initiatives have been effective? Which demographics in your employee base think DEIB training has been successful? Which ones do not?

- **Policies** – Has training helped you understand and then modify policies that weren't inclusive and equitable?

It is crucial to have your eyes open and continue to work to see what is successful and what isn't. Further, training and learning should never be considered done. DEIB training is like eating or breathing—we need it to sustain a healthy existence.

I know; I can feel the glare. How much training on DEIB could there be? And how on earth do you continue to provide learning opportunities or ongoing comprehensive training without breaking the bank or losing the buy-in from every level? After all, we see what happens with the canned videos and multiple-choice tests we do every year.

Well—again, I am so glad you asked!

Ongoing Comprehensive Training

The business case for ongoing comprehensive DEIB training isn't a hard one to make. First, the subject of DEI is so vast and colorful that you would be hard-pressed to repeatedly go over the same material. Second, we have learned that authentic DEI leads to better employee retention and satisfaction. Not to mention the corporate bottom line benefits.

So, what type of training can you offer and why? Let's look at a description of the multitude of training options and their importance, shall we?

- **The Business Case for Diversity**: Yes! There is training for making the business case for diversity. If you have difficulty getting the buy-in, this is where to start! Learning the facts and having the data helps you speak confidently about the subject and why you need a DEI initiative.

- **Navigating the DEI Journey:** Building an inclusive organization is a journey, not a destination. In this training, participants explore the intricacies of this ongoing journey with confidence. From assessing current practices to developing a strategic plan, attendees learn how to navigate the complexities of Diversity, Equity, and Inclusion (DEI) initiatives. The training emphasizes the importance of incorporating a change management plan tailored to the organization's unique tolerance for change. By understanding and addressing these dynamics, participants are equipped to build a culture where everyone feels valued, respected, and included.

- **DEI's Impact on Organizational Success** – Ever wondered how Diversity, Equity, and Inclusion (DEI) initiatives can truly transform your organization? Well, wonder no more. This training is all about unlocking the full potential of DEI to drive success – internally and externally. We're not just talking about checking off boxes here; we're talking about making a real impact. From fostering a more inclusive culture to boosting productivity and profits, DEI has the power to revolutionize your organization. And it's not just about what happens inside your company walls – DEI can also strengthen relationships with customers, drive economic impact, and build bridges with external stakeholders. It's time to turn DEI from a buzzword into a game-changer for your organization.

- **Unconscious Bias Training:** This training is a BIG one and helps employees recognize the assumptions and judgments they make about people based on their appearance or background. It's important to note that everyone has biases and that these biases can impact decisions made in the workplace. When we train on the subject, we focus on four areas: Origination, Workplace Culture, Organization, and Individual Responsibility. We work to explore how implicit bias is influenced by history and social norms. Then we question how it shows up in the workplace. From there, we work on helping the organization identify its role in minimizing implicit bias. Finally, we help leaders and employees discover their roles in reducing bias.

- **Intersectionality Training:** This type of training explores how different types of discrimination (e.g., racism, sexism, homophobia) intersect and impact individuals who belong to multiple marginalized groups. We so often think that discrimination is a Black or white issue. We fail to see that it isn't that simple. When we explore how discrimination intersects, you might be surprised by how prevalent it can be.

- **Micro-Aggressions Training:** Micro-aggressions are everyday slights, insults, or comments that can be based on someone's race, gender, sexual orientation, or another status. This type of training can help employees identify micro-aggressions and understand their impact on others. We often try to wave off micro-aggressions—it was just a joke—why are you so sensitive—I wasn't serious. Sound familiar? Have you heard it? What about the cliques in the workplace? Could they be micro-aggressions?

- **Becoming an Inclusive Leader:** Leadership isn't just about calling the shots – it's also about creating an environment where everyone feels included and valued. In this training, you'll develop the skills and mindset you need to lead inclusively. From creating psychologically safe spaces to empowering diverse teams, you'll learn how to drive real change and build a culture of inclusion.

- **DEI and Emotional Intelligence:** Ever wonder how emotions tie into creating an inclusive workplace? This training dives deep into that. It's all about understanding and managing emotions to build strong relationships across diverse teams. You'll learn to navigate different perspectives and communicate effectively, all while fostering an environment where everyone feels heard and valued.

- **Fostering a Culture of Inclusion and Belonging:** This training empowers both leaders and individual contributors to play active roles in shaping a workplace culture that embraces diversity and promotes inclusivity. Participants delve into the dynamics of inclusion and belonging, recognizing that true inclusivity involves creating an environment where psychological safety thrives and individuals feel comfortable expressing their authentic selves without fear of retribution. Through interactive discussions and practical strategies, attendees gain the tools to cultivate a culture where everyone feels respected, valued, and able to contribute their unique perspectives.

- **Disability and DEI:** This training focuses on raising awareness about the diverse range of disabilities, including both visible and invisible disabilities. It sheds light on the experiences of individuals with disabilities, addressing unconscious biases and the various obstacles they encounter in the workplace. By fostering understanding and empathy, the training aims to improve conditions and relationships, ultimately fostering a sense of belonging for individuals with disabilities.

- **Multigenerational Workforce:** As workplaces become more diverse, it's important to recognize and appreciate the perspectives and needs of employees spanning multiple generations. This training equips employees with the understanding and skills needed to collaborate effectively across generational divides, fostering a more inclusive and harmonious work environment.

- **LGBTQ+:** This training offers insights into the unique experiences and challenges faced by lesbian, gay, bisexual, transgender, and queer individuals in the workplace. By increasing understanding and empathy, this training fosters a more inclusive environment where all employees feel respected and valued for who they are.

- **Supporting Gender Identity and Expression:** This training helps employees understand the importance of inclusion for employees of all gender identities and expressions. It explores best practices for fostering inclusivity in language, policies, and practices, as well as strategies for advocating for gender-affirming environments.

- **Neurodiversity in the Workplace:** This training helps employees understand the needs of employees with neurodiverse conditions such as ADHD, dyslexia, and autism. It can also help employees to learn how to accommodate neurodiverse employees in the workplace.

- **Recruiting and Hiring from a DEI lens:** Hiring diverse talent isn't just the right thing to do – it's also good for business. In this training, get the tools and strategies needed to recruit and hire with diversity and inclusion in mind. From crafting inclusive job descriptions to minimizing bias during the interview processes, learn how to attract and select candidates who bring unique perspectives to the table.

- **Developing an Equitable Promotion Process:** Want to make sure everyone has a fair shot at advancement? This training is a must for leaders. Learn how to identify and address systemic barriers to promotion, create objective evaluation criteria, and promote equity in career development opportunities. It's all about creating a level playing field where everyone has an opportunity to succeed.

- **Courageous Conversations**: Let's face it – talking about diversity and inclusion can be uncomfortable. But it doesn't have to be. This training empowers participants to engage in open, honest, and respectful discussions about DEI topics. Through interactive exercises and guided dialogue, attendees learn how to navigate challenging conversations surrounding race, gender, privilege, and other sensitive issues while leveraging the power of polarity thinking. By understanding the dynamics of "both/and" thinking versus "either/or" thinking, participants can seek win-win solutions that honor diverse perspectives and foster inclusivity. This approach encourages individuals to embrace courage and vulnerability, enabling them to initiate and sustain meaningful conversations that drive positive change within their organizations and communities.

- **Cultivating Cultural Sensitivity:** This training enhances participants' awareness of personal biases and perspectives that can hinder acceptance of others. Participants develop skills in awareness, curiosity, and clarity to navigate cultural diversity with respect and understanding. By fostering empathy and humility, participants learn to appreciate the nuances of different cultural perspectives, fostering inclusive environments where everyone feels valued and respected.

- **From Allyship to Collaboration:** This training guides participants on a journey from passive allyship to active collaboration in fostering DE). Participants learn how to move beyond symbolic gestures and towards meaningful actions that drive positive change. Participants explore strategies for building authentic relationships, amplifying diverse voices, and co-creating inclusive spaces. By embracing collaboration, attendees are empowered to become proactive agents of change.

- **Healing Circles Facilitation:** This training focuses on creating safe spaces for healing and reconciliation in the context of DEI efforts. Participants learn facilitation techniques, active listening skills, and trauma-informed practices to support individuals and communities in processing and healing from past traumas.

- **DEI Train the Trainer Program:** This training equips participants with the knowledge and skills to effectively facilitate DEI training sessions within their organizations. Through experiential learning, feedback sessions, and peer collaboration, participants become certified DEI trainers capable of driving meaningful change and fostering inclusive learning environments.

As you can see, a wide range of DEIB training is available, and these are just a few—each with its own important focus. The key is to find the right mix for your organization and offer ongoing training that covers various topics. By doing so, you can create a genuinely inclusive workplace for all. And when you focus and commit to ongoing comprehensive training, you will find that your DEIB efforts pay off. What you give time to will gain momentum.

REFLECTION AND APPLICATION

- Has your DEIB training failed in the past? If so, why do you think so?
- Do you currently offer any experiential learning or training?
- What DEIB training do you see as a priority for your organization?

CHAPTER 8

WHAT YOU FOCUS ON WILL EXPAND

> *"What you focus on grows, what you think about expands, and what you dwell on determines your destiny."*
> ~ Robin S. Sharma

In This Chapter

- Policies and Practices
- Recruiting, hiring, onboarding, compensation, promotion, workplace policies
- DEIB Metrics
- Reflection and Application

There are several quotes like the title and passage of this chapter. You've probably even heard the quote from Peter Druker, "what gets measured, gets managed." We see it time and again.

However, the selection is the perfect example of the telephone game. Druker admittedly never said it. Instead, it was V. F. Ridgway, in a 1956 paper titled *Dysfunctional Consequences of Performance Measurements*. The correct quote is,

> "What gets measured gets managed—even when it's pointless to measure and manage it, and even if it harms the purpose of the organization to do so."

Well, I am not sure about you, but this was an eye-opener for many! All the years you were convinced that you needed to measure it, so it gets managed—only to find out it is complete dysfunction. Palm plant to face—*sigh*.

Have you seen how it works? A directive comes from above. Maybe this month, it's the employee's customer utilization rate or how many calls are completed. The thing is, you have to be mindful of what you are measuring because there can be unintended consequences if you are not careful—because whatever it is—will expand. Perhaps, just not how you intended. There are endless stories of how focusing on the wrong thing for the wrong reason turns out badly. Has the 911 operator story enlightened you yet? The short version is that the staff at a British outsourced Police call center control room "were making 999 calls at quiet times in order to meet their target of answering 92% of calls within 10 seconds."[41]

Now, can you imagine! Technically, they got the job done. But yikes! Not really what you want from an emergency call center, or is it just me?

The point is, you need to be mindful of what you focus on and know what you want to expand—preferable before changing policies and practices just to change policies and practices.

We touched on this subject slightly in discussing the business case and best practices. However, DEIB policies, practices, and metrics are the lifeline of your DEIB effort. If they are wrong, your effort will fail. From Recruiting, Hiring, and Onboarding to compensation, promotions, and advancements—your workplace policies and DEIB metrics need to focus on your DEIB objectives. So, let's dig in a little deeper so you can gain a better perspective.

Let's start with getting candidates in the door, hired, and onboarded adequately.

Recruiting, Hiring, and Onboarding

The first way to set your DEIB policies, practices, and metrics is by looking at your recruiting, hiring, and onboarding process. If you want a more diverse workforce, you must ensure that your

---

[41] https://www.theguardian.com/uk-news/2016/may/23/g4s-police-control-room-staff-suspended-claims-bogus-999-calls-lincolnshire-force

recruiting practices reach a diverse pool of potential candidates. This means posting job openings in places where people of color and other underrepresented groups will see them. It also means conducting outreach to organizations that focus on these groups. You can also work with staffing agencies that specialize in diversity recruitment. For example, did you know there are recruiting agencies specializing in second chance hiring? Second chance hiring is the practice of hiring those with a criminal background. Did you know that one-third of working-age US adults have a criminal record?[42] The key is to understand that you have to think outside the box and connect in ways you have never considered before.

Another area to put under the microscope is your job duties and descriptions for positions. Our unconscious bias gets in the way far too often. For example, you may have a job requiring heavy lifting monthly. You may needlessly be excluding well-qualified candidates because of this one nuance.[43] Reconsider whether you can get someone else to do the heavy lifting when needed.

Further, look at your job postings to see whom you are attracting. If you have the words like high-energy or energetic go-getter—is that really what you need? An introvert might be perfectly capable without all the rah-rah.

When it comes to your hiring process, studies have shown that interviewers often give preferential treatment to candidates like them. To combat this, consider using blind resumes or structured interviews focusing on specific skills and qualifications rather than relying on the interviewer's gut feeling. Online skills

---

[42] https://www.shrm.org/executive/resources/articles/pages/blog-second-chance-employment-janove.aspx
[43] https://crescendowork.com/guide-start-diversity-inclusion-strategy/2019/2/26/diversity-inclusion-audit-processes-structures-policies#recruiting-process

tests are sometimes used to remove bias. Finally, you can provide training to your interviewers on how to avoid unconscious bias.

Once you've made an offer to a candidate, it's crucial to set them up for success from the start by providing a comprehensive onboarding experience. This should include an overview of company culture, expectations for the role, and resources for getting acclimated to the workplace. For employees of color and other underrepresented groups, consider offering additional support through mentorship programs or employee resource groups. It is about giving them a warm sense of belonging from the beginning. However, remember the previous discussions—it must be authentic, and candidates should never feel "tokenized."

Compensation

Your compensation policies and practices are another important area concerning DEIB. Studies have shown that people of color and women are often paid less than their white male counterparts. To combat this, consider conducting a pay equity analysis to ensure everyone is paid fairly for their position and experience level. You can also institute policies prohibiting asking candidates about their current or previous salaries.

Promotions and Advancements

When it comes to promotions and advancements, again, studies have shown that people of color and women are often passed over in favor of white men. To address this issue, consider implementing policies that focus on merit-based advancement. This means basing promotions and raises on an employee's job performance rather than length of time with the company or personal connections. You can also create opportunities for employees to stretch themselves professionally by offering assignments outside their typical job descriptions.

General Workplace Policies

Your general workplace policies will speak volumes about your DEIB effort. Workplace policies play a crucial role in shaping the culture and environment of an organization. They not only outline expectations and procedures but also reflect the organization's commitment to fostering inclusivity, fairness, and respect for all employees.

In addition to fundamental policies addressing conduct, health, safety, and discrimination, inclusive workplace policies are essential for creating an environment where every individual feels valued, supported, and empowered.

Let's explore a comprehensive range of inclusive policies that can contribute to building a diverse, equitable, and inclusive workplace:

- **Comprehensive parental leave policies:** Recognizing both maternity and paternity needs to ensure equal opportunities for all caregivers.

- **Holiday policies review:** Accommodating diverse religious and cultural observances to prevent discrimination and exclusion.

- **Flexible working arrangements:** Supporting diverse needs and responsibilities through flexible work schedules and remote work options.

- **Work-life balance initiatives:** Promoting balance with flexible hours, compressed workweeks, and parental leave policies.

- **Employee resource groups (ERGs):** Providing platforms for employees from diverse backgrounds to come together, share experiences, and advocate for inclusivity.

- **Feedback mechanisms:** Gathering insights into employees' experiences and concerns to improve workplace policies and practices.

- **Language accessibility:** Supporting employees and customers whose first language isn't English with translation services and language training programs.

- **Dignity at work:** Prohibiting bullying, harassment, discrimination, and disrespectful behavior with clear reporting and addressing procedures.

- **Sexual harassment policies:** Establishing zero-tolerance policies and procedures for reporting and addressing incidents.

- **Disability accommodations:** Ensuring equal opportunities with reasonable accommodations and accessibility enhancements.

- **Diversity and Inclusion Training:** Raising awareness of unconscious bias and fostering an inclusive mindset across the organization.

- **Transparent Pay Practices:** Ensuring fairness and equity in compensation with transparent pay policies and regular equity audits.

- **Career Development Opportunities:** Providing equitable access to advancement opportunities and mentorship programs.

- **Inclusive Recruitment and Hiring Practices:** Prioritizing diversity, equity, and inclusion in recruitment and hiring processes.

- **Pronoun Inclusivity:** Affirming employees' gender identities with gender-inclusive language and pronoun options.

- **Employee Assistance Programs (EAPs):** Supporting mental health and well-being with comprehensive counseling services and resources.

- **Family-Friendly Policies:** Accommodating diverse family structures and life stages with childcare benefits and lactation rooms.

- **Inclusive Benefits Packages:** Meeting diverse needs with comprehensive healthcare coverage and support for fertility treatments.

- **Environmental Sustainability Policies:** Promoting eco-friendly practices and social responsibility through sustainability initiatives.

- **Supplier Diversity Initiatives:** Supporting economic equity and diversity by partnering with underrepresented businesses.

Metrics

Finally, it's essential to have DEIB-focused metrics in place to track your progress and ensure that your policies and practices actually have the desired effect. Of course, you might wonder what DEIB metrics are and what metrics you should track. So, let's take a look!

DEIB metrics are the numerical measurements used to track the progress of your DEIB effort. This could include anything from the percentage of employees from underrepresented groups to the number of harassment complaints or discrimination. By tracking these metrics, you can gauge whether or not your policies and practices are making a difference in creating a more diverse and inclusive workplace.

Your DEIB metrics should encompass five areas: recruitment, retention, advancement, representation, and pay.[44] You may have noticed that Supplier DEIB metrics are missing. Well, they get their own chapter! Here are some examples of DEIB metrics that you may want to track include:

- Percentage of employees from underrepresented groups
- Percentage of new hires from underrepresented groups
- What is your attrition rate at each level of the organization
- Number of complaints of harassment or discrimination
- Percentage of employees who feel they have opportunities for advancement
- Percentage of employees who feel they are paid fairly
- Percentage of employees who feel they are treated with respect

---

[44] https://www.bcg.com/capabilities/diversity-inclusion/measuring-diversity-equity-inclusion

- Percentage of promotions or advancements given to employees from underrepresented groups
- Percentage of employees who feel like they have an equal opportunity to succeed at the company
- Percentage of employees who believe pay levels are equitable

Now, you can always reinvent the wheel and create your own surveys, DEIB tracking system, and policies. Or you can seek out all the examples, resources, and tools available. Creating or revamping your DEIB program doesn't have to be done alone. As a matter of fact, it shouldn't. Remember that organizational culture bias? The point is to get a new perspective. So, consider your options.

REFLECTION AND APPLICATION

- Are you currently aware of any discriminatory policies or practices in your organization?
- When is the last time you read through job postings or descriptions through a DEIB lens?
- Do you currently have any DEIB metrics? If so, are you making progress, or do you know?

CHAPTER 9

SUPPLIER DIVERSITY

> *"If you want to lift yourself up, lift up someone else."*
> ~ Booker T. Washington

In This Chapter

- Benefits & Importance of Supplier Diversity Development
- Advancing Supply Chain Diversity Through a Supplier DEIB Program
- Reflection and Application

"On average, suppler diversity programs add $3.6 million to the bottom line for every $1 million in procurement operation costs."[45]

---

[45] https://www.supplier.io/blog/supplier-diversity-programs-vs.-supplier-development-programs#:~:text=Research%20shows%20that%20companies%20that,study%20by%20The%20Hackett%20Group.

This is only one of the benefits of supplier chain diversity. We touch on others in previous chapters. However, it cannot be emphasized enough the vast reach supply chain diversity has from the organization to the community and back. So, let's break it down!

Did you know that according to the 2021 Census Annual Business Survey (ABS), "approximately 18.3% (1.0 million) of all US businesses were minority-owned and about 19.9% (1.1 million) of all businesses were owned by women. Veteran-owned businesses made up about 5.9% of all businesses, with an estimated $947.7 billion in receipts, 3.9 million employees, and about $177.7 billion in annual payroll."?[46] Further, research led by American Express in 2019 revealed that "an impressive four million new jobs and $981 billion in revenue could be added to the American economy if the average revenue of minority women-owned businesses matched those of white women-owned businesses."[47] This is nothing to sneeze at!

Benefits & Importance of Supplier Diversity Development

When you look at the numbers, we see billions of dollars in revenue and payroll. Payroll gets pushed into the economy—rent, food, gas, cars, furniture, clothes, dining out, and other consumables. So, supporting these businesses is vital.

---

[46] https://www.census.gov/newsroom/press-releases/2021/annual-business-survey.html

[47] https://www.jdsupra.com/legalnews/the-importance-of-vendor-diversity-5316562/#:~:text=Vendor%20diversity%20really%20is%20an,happier%20local%20and%20vendor%20community

But perhaps even more important is helping **develop** supplier diversity. Why so?

First, you can improve supply chain transparency, gain a competitive advantage, and foster loyalty. Developing a supplier inevitably exposes them to other buyers, increasing competition between buyers and resulting in improved services and better rates. Further, when you establish trust and a one-on-one relationship with your suppliers, they will most likely look out for you before others. For example, they may warn you of disruptions early, like during the pandemic and global supply disruptions. If you had a mask supplier, they might have warned you of shortages and allocated limited resources to you first.[48]

Second, we know diversity drives innovation. However, your supplier may have the potential but not the resources to take advantage of that innovation. Providing network access and mentoring could help get them over the hurdles.

Finally, when you help to develop supplier diversity, your organization may have a hand in improving quality and building your corporate social responsibility cred. When you are involved at a deeper level, you can help address and resolve issues with quality control. Further, when you help improve their organization by becoming more innovative and productive, you benefit their local community through job creation and economic growth.

So how do you advance supplier diversity in the supply chain? Great question!

Advancing Supplier Diversity in the Supply Chain

It's all about procurement—having a strategic plan that includes diverse suppliers—and procurement starts with leadership buy-in.

---

[48] https://www.thomasnet.com/insights/supplier-development/

Now, you think—*but I already got leadership buy-in for our DEIB initiative.* Maybe so. However, did you specifically get buy-in for supplier diversity?? Well—did you?

Ahhh—yes. I ask because I know. Only about ten percent of COOs and about eighteen of CEOs and boards show support for these programs even when they support DEIB internally.[49] There is a disconnect. If you have buy-in on supplier diversity development—congratulate yourself! If not, move back three spaces and get the buy-in—you cannot go forward without it!

A supplier diversity program begins with and flows in the same way your internal DEIB effort does. To start, if you don't have executive sponsorship, you need to build a business case. These two go hand in hand. If you skipped over the steps in the previous chapter for building a DEIB program, here's a quick rundown specific to your supplier DEIB effort. There are best practices that will help organize and manage your supplier development.

Best Practices for Establishing a Supplier Diversity Program

First, let's talk about the accepted gold standard for diversity program development. This would be the Five Levels of Supplier Diversity Program Development from Ralph Moore, the president of Ralph G. Moore and Associates (RGMA). This is the standard for benchmarking corporate supplier diversity initiatives.

---

[49] https://www.supplyshift.net/advancing-diversity-equity-and-inclusion-in-your-supply-chain

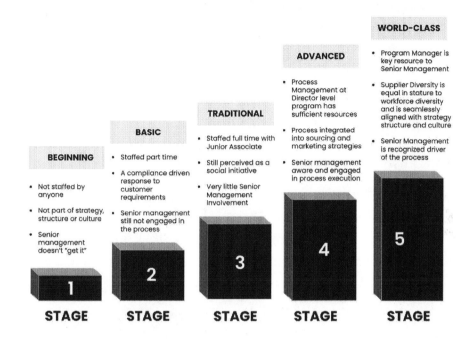

Source: RGMA's Five Levels of Supplier Diversity Program Development, by Ralph G. Moore

Starting at ground zero, you have no formal program. From there, you can see how your benchmarks will or should progress as you continue to build your program. Notice the divide between levels zero through three. Organizations will often get stuck at level three and fail to progress to levels four and five. We touched on the myths, misconceptions, and barriers that can block forward movement on internal DEIB progress. The same goes for a Supplier Diversity Program.

You must go through many of the same steps to get past the barriers.

- **Step1. Establish the Business Case secure Executive Sponsorship** – Provide accurate and up-to-date information on the benefits and importance of supplier diversity and secure leadership support.

- **Step 2. Perform a Current State Assessment** – Do an audit of your suppliers to create a DEIB baseline. This could include sending surveys to your supplier leadership and opening a line of communication for feedback. Ask questions and collect data that align with what you hope to accomplish.

- **Step 3. Develop a Governance Model** – Will you create a supplier DEIB committee? How will you monitor and manage your supplier development? Will you include members of your supplier leadership in the model? Their participation is needed and valuable.

- **Step 4. Create a Supplier Diversity Policy** – Similar to your organizational DEIB statement, you want to establish a supplier statement addressing DEIB. What are your goals? What do you hope to accomplish? Talk with current or potential suppliers and ask what they need. Your goals and objectives might differ—if they are, your supplier DEIB efforts could fall flat. Align with, and support supplier needs and goals. For example, if you and your supplier want to reduce costs or improve performance, you have aligned goals. However, if you are looking for cost reductions and your supplier wants to innovate new products, you might need to have a conversation.

- **Step 5. Establish Metrics** – Once you audit and have a baseline, you need to set metrics to help measure progress towards your objectives and supplier diversity goals.

There are three metrics that you want to be sure you have in place. They are direct impact, indirect impact, and induced impact. Your direct impact metrics will measure what is spent on goods, services, and jobs created with your diverse supplier. Indirect impact is the measure of the growth in diversity in suppliers and revenues in the supply chain. Finally, induced impact will measure the wider economic benefit to the local economy based on the direct and indirect impact.[50]

- **Step 6. Prepare and Create a Change Management Plan** – First, you need to review the status of your relationships with suppliers and availability of suppliers, as well as the organizational willingness to start or expand supplier diversity. You have to consider that many buyers and prime suppliers say they can't find qualified suppliers or are high risk. Further, they often have a solid relationship with the incumbent non-minority suppliers that may serve as 2nd/3rd tier suppliers. This means a lot of extra homework and possibly taking existing work from strategic partners and suppliers they've had long-standing relationships with—friends, etc. Second, you may need a change management plan to work with leaders, buyers, and other stakeholders who embrace a Supplier Diversity initiative.

The change management plan will help with supplier and buyer internal changes. For the first, if you find your current suppliers aren't as diverse, you have to consider if

---

[50] https://www.gep.com/blog/mind/turning-supplier-diversity-programs-into-a-competitive-advantage#:~:text=The%20economic%20impact%20of%20supplier%20diversity%20can%20be%20measured%20with,across%20the%20entire%20supply%20chain

they are willing and able to change and participate. If not, you need a process for establishing relationships with new suppliers. For the second, if you have a willing supplier, they might not have the resources or know how to implement the needed changes. How will you help? Remember, for smaller businesses, the DEIB effort can be resource-intensive and time-consuming. For both, a good start is to institute policies where at least one minority supplier has to be included in bids and tie performance bonuses to supplier diversity goals.

For a change management plan to be successful, you want to consider the following:

- o Share your supplier diversity goals with your employees through different media outlets to get them involved.
- o Ask for employee feedback on your goals and initiatives. An open line of communication with employees can shed light on their enthusiasm or lack thereof.
- o Promote your diversity efforts and share on social media. Share successes of onboarding diverse suppliers.
- o Encourage Patronage to Diverse Suppliers. Share lists of diverse suppliers so that employees can support them more easily.

- **Step 7. Develop a Communications Plan** – Your supplier diversity program doesn't exist if it isn't communicated properly or consistently. You will need a chain of communication internally between you and your suppliers, one with each supplier individually, and may even need to help them with their communication plan. Your communication plan needs to include all internal buyers, leaders, stakeholders, external suppliers, and the community. You want to make sure there is a feedback loop that stays open.

Now, you may also need to incentivize your suppliers to stay engaged. How you incentive engagement will depend on any rules or policies in place that could be seen negatively. For example, some industries might see incentives as kickbacks. If you know, you know!

You want to be sure to explain not only goals or objectives but also the trends and numbers. You need to connect the relevance of the numbers and statistics to the impact they will have. Tie to the WIFM. This might be reducing costs, job creation and increase innovation. The message must match the WIFM. Finally, remember it isn't all about the numbers; you have to go beyond that to the brand loyalty the program can create.

- **Step 8. Create a Training Strategy** – Do your suppliers have the resources for training? Could you bring suppliers together for training at regular intervals? Training is a great way to get in the door and build relationships within the supplier ecosystem. Engaging with them on their turf shows you genuinely care about what they do and how they progress on their own goals. Anytime you can authentically engage, do!

  Your training strategy should also include training for corporate leaders, supplier diversity managers, supply chain, buyers, primes, etc. The training should show how diverse suppliers strengthen the supply chain and the process for incorporating more diverse suppliers in the supply chain. The goal of Supplier Development is first to get leadership on board; then they will champion it to internal buyers who intern will open up contract opportunities to diverse suppliers and encourage primes (who are probably not diverse) to include diverse suppliers in joint venture/strategic partnership opportunities or provide opportunities to serve as a 2nd or 3rd tier suppliers.

- **Step 9. Develop a Sourcing Strategy** – Your sourcing strategy should first work to look internally to see what diverse suppliers you have in the pipeline, those that you are already doing business with, and where you can increase spend. Then, figure out where you are spending your procurement. You want to broaden your procurement pool within the categories you already spend. Finally, be sure you have implemented the "rule of one" mentioned above. Be sure that every bid has at least one diverse supplier bidder.[51]

Now, if your current suppliers aren't willing to participate in your initiative, you need a strategy for sourcing suppliers committed to DEIB and corporate social responsibility. Will you have a point person who will engage in nonprofits or trade groups for businesses owned by underrepresented groups? What about community outreach? Where will you connect with other suppliers and companies who support your effort? Could you spearhead a local business community group on the subject?

---

[51] https://www.forbes.com/sites/forbesbusinesscouncil/2021/08/06/why-diverse-and-inclusive-supply-chains-are-needed-and-three-tips-to-make-it-happen/?sh=e16dc7c60f10

- **Step 10. Develop a Supplier Development Program** – Consider formalizing your supplier development program with a clear and defined process. For example, which suppliers will you bring into the fold? What are the selection criteria? How will you prioritize whom you select? What will you offer in the program? Will you have a formal induction and ongoing milestones that have to be kept?

    Further, coaching and mentoring are essential. Do you have a mentor or coaching plan? Finally, do you have access to decision-makers for participation in RFPs aligned with their business products or services? You want to set rules for the game. It can't be a free for all.

Now, if this all sounds like a lot of work, it is!

What, you thought I would lie and tell you it's all puppies and butterflies? No. Nothing of value comes that easily. And frankly, we have to help uncoil the messes we have made. I can tell you that a company free from bias or discrimination doesn't exist. Even the good ones with robust DEIB programs still have issues. It is because we are human. We are never perfect—and there is always something to learn, understand, or try to make sense of. We are constantly evolving—and that is good so long as we learn the lessons and take steps to improve.

If you are still slightly unconvinced, I leave you with this:

"Supplier diversity is evolving from a check-the-box corporate social responsibility requirement to a strategic enabler providing access to innovative products and increased market share in new and developing communities. Top-performing organizations are taking advantage of this opportunity and applying the tenets of social diversity

to new areas such as supplier partnering, reputation management, and global expansion with exceptional results."
—Laura Gibbons, Research Director, The Hackett Group—
Inga Beale.

Some get it, and some don't. Will you be left behind, or will you get on board?

REFLECTION AND APPLICATION

- Do you already have executive support for a supplier diversity program?
- Have you worked through the steps of establishing a supplier effort?
- Do you have supplier buy-in or willing participants?
- What hurdles do you face trying to implement a supplier diversity program?

CHAPTER 10

MOVING BEYOND DIVERSITY TO INCLUSION AND BELONGING

> *"A deep sense of love and belonging is an irreducible need of all people. We are biologically, cognitively, physically, and spiritually wired to love, to be loved, and to belong. When those needs are not met, we don't function as we were meant to. We break. We fall apart. We numb. We ache. We hurt others. We get sick."*
>
> ~ Brene Brown

In This Chapter

- Diversity to Equity
- Culture of Inclusion
- Belonging is the Missing Piece
- Reflection and Application

We have spent much of the book focused on Diversity, Equity, and Inclusion. After all, that is what is politically correct. It is what we are told we need to focus on. Our profits and bottom line depend on it. Our credibility depends on it. Our employees and community depend on it. Throughout history, we have focused and worked for an understanding of diversity, demanding equity and inclusion. In many ways, we have achieved all three. However, there has always been a piece of the puzzle that was missing. Maybe under the table or lost in the shuffle on the closet. It sits patiently waiting to join—to complete the picture, the vision. We often work so hard to complete the DEIB masterpiece but leave out one vital ingredient—a sense of belonging.

Diversity, equity, and inclusion are not the same as belonging. And, if your DEIB efforts have failed, I would say it is because you failed in belonging.

Diversity to Inclusion

To understand, we need to explore the nuance. First, diversity and inclusion are separate and completely different concepts. However, both are essential for the emotional experience we know as that sense of belonging. You can't have one or the other—you must have both. But what are they exactly? I know we think we know. But do we?

Let's start with diversity. Diversity by definition is "variety" or "multiformity." Diversity is a state of existence—it is a fact. It's about being different. And it's not just about being of different races and ethnicities, though that is part of it. As we have discovered, it's also about being of different genders, ages, religions, socio-economic backgrounds, sexual orientations, abilities, and disabilities. In short, diversity is about who we are—how we differ.

It is not enough to BE different or know that everyone IS different. We have to expand our thinking beyond that acknowledgment. We must work to accept, embrace, understand, and celebrate differences. For example, it is not enough to know you have co-workers who don't celebrate Christmas or that the guy down the hall is neurodiverse. To tell your children we all look different when she asks about a person in a wheelchair stops a little short.

After all, remember your history. Segregation laws acknowledged that we are different.

This is where equity comes in. We eventually realized that acknowledging differences was not enough. We had to work towards equity. Now equity doesn't equal equality. Equity is about creating fair access—leveling the playing field. Equity isn't just about opening the door.

Source: *Equity vs. Equality*. Northwestern Health Unit

See the difference?

Culture of Inclusion

Then there is inclusion. Inclusion means to include. Inclusive is action—it is behavior. The thing is, we can include those that are different from us without them feeling included. We can give equal access, but it doesn't mean there is equity. Does that make sense?

Think about it. We can invite someone to a party but not make them feel included. We can put someone on a team but not give them equal opportunities to contribute. We can go through the motions of being inclusive without actually being inclusive.

Inclusion is not about the invite. It's about creating an environment where everyone feels like they are valued and respected. It's about ensuring that everyone has the opportunity to participate and contribute. It's about ensuring everyone has a seat at the table, and their voice is heard. It's also about ensuring that people with diverse perspectives are included in the conversation so that we can make better decisions. It's about removing barriers, creating equity, and making sure everyone feels like they are wanted—that they belong.

And that sense of belonging is essential for all of us. It's what allows us to show up as our best selves. It's what gives us the courage to take risks and be vulnerable. And it's what will enable us to build relationships and trust.

Did you know that exclusion actually harms performance and can physically cause pain? In 2011, a Purdue professor of psychological sciences reported:

> "Being excluded or ostracized is an invisible form of bullying that doesn't leave bruises, and therefore we often underestimate its impact." He goes on to say, "Being excluded by high school friends, office colleagues, or even spouses or family members can be excruciating. And because ostracism is experienced in three stages, the life of those painful feelings can be extended for the long term. People and clinicians need to be aware of this so they can avoid depression or other negative experiences."[52]

Brain images show that the part of the brain that feels physical pain lights up when being excluded. This is because being excluded takes aim at our fundamental needs of self-esteem and belonging.

When it comes to performance, those who have been excluded respond in two ways. The first is trying to fit in. They will work to conform or comply. The second is to reject the group and find acceptance elsewhere. Now, it doesn't take a wild sense of imagination to envision where either response can lead.

On the one hand, you will have those that fall in line conform to the norm and keep their head down. All the while, they are miserable and quite literally in pain. They will be the ones that might even allow themselves to be the butt of the joke, act as the

---

[52] https://www.purdue.edu/newsroom/research/2011/110510WilliamsOstracism.html

office jester, or become vulnerable to unwanted advances or taken advantage of by other means. On the other hand, you could watch one of your best employees isolate and eventually leave for greener pasture.

For all these reasons, your organization needs to work past the typical diversity, equity, and inclusion narrative. It is time to go beyond the traditional half-hearted attempts at DEIB and find ways to bring a sense of belonging.

Belonging is the Missing Piece

Take a moment and think of a time you felt excluded. We have all had them. Maybe when you were a kid and didn't get invited to the birthday party. Perhaps you were lucky and didn't experience exclusion or rejection until high school when you didn't make the football or debate team. I can almost bet that everyone felt excluded as a new employee at a company. You walk into the break room and get the odd looks, the whispers—no? If you can't recall one single time, I would challenge you to think harder.

Now, think about that moment. How you felt. Maybe sad, alone—even desperate to try and fit in—like you would do anything if they would just let you join. Of course, as adults, we learn to redirect emotions or temper them. But in many ways, when we are excluded, we go through those same feelings.

Take that and imagine it on the daily. Not fun.

Now, take a minute and think about the warm feeling deep in your bones when you have been genuinely welcomed into a group—that time when they embraced you, you were given a voice—the opportunity to be heard and participate. You felt safe and even confident. You feel like you can accomplish what you set out to do because you have support. You feel you can maybe take a little more risk because you are accepted and encouraged.

Which do you want your employees to feel? I know it seems obvious. But—do they feel that way? You can't wish it so.

How do you create a sense of belonging that reverberates through the organization? It isn't easy, and there is no direct or 'right' path to take. But if you start with empathy, it is a great beginning.

It Begins with Empathy

Empathy literally means to 'suffer with.' It is the ability to be aware, sensitive, and understand how someone else feels or what it is like to be in their situation. Empathy takes a slightly higher level of emotional intelligence. The good thing is that we are all capable of empathy. For example, the little exercise I went through at the beginning of this section—asking you to think of a time you felt excluded and how it made you feel—is an exercise in empathy. Put yourself in someone else's shoes.

Here's the thing. We all have empathy when we are children. However, as we grow, life gets in the way, we become jaded and busy—and we detach from our ability to empathize. We must begin prioritizing life and emotions, and showing empathy to our ever-expanding network of humans can be draining. Our detachment is often out of survival. We have to be selective in whom we offer empathy. Our co-workers should be one of those we prioritize.

Just with diversity, empathy enhances well-being and productivity throughout an organization. So, here are a few teams centered empathy exercises[53] to build that empathetic muscle:

---

[53] https://www.ringcentral.com/us/en/blog/empathy-exercises/

Active listening – Have you ever heard you have two ears and one mouth—use them accordingly. It means we should listen more than we speak. However, we need to listen ACTIVELY. You can bring your team (or teams) together and pick a conversational topic. Everyone pairs up and has a dialog. The speaker will share their story, and the listener will listen and then restate what they heard and ask questions for more details. Then they switch.

You may have engaged in this exercise at team building or training seminars. It is some version of finding someone not sitting next to you and introducing yourself and discovering something interesting about them. Everyone takes ten to twenty minutes and then has to share what they learned about that person, what they got right, or what was left out.

Active listening is about having engaging and in-depth conversations.

Devil's Advocate – This exercise is about taking a situation and flipping what you believe to be right and taking the point of view. It could be the angry and unreasonable customer that insists they are right. Perhaps they are being irrational. It is your job to uncover why they feel this way and find why what they are experiencing may not be irrational or unreasonable.

We never know both sides of the story unless we listen and try to see things from someone else's perspective. We never know what someone is going through. Maybe they recently had a death in the family, or they are going through a divorce. Perhaps they lost their job or found out they have cancer. Or it could be their newborn baby kept them up all night.

This is not to say we make excuses for abusive behavior. However, we can show empathy and understanding for the situation or their feelings.

This or That – The great thing about this exercise is that there are no right or wrong answers. It is purely about perception and working to understand how and why someone will view something differently than you. One of the most recent and popular examples of the 'this or that' exercise took social media by storm a few years ago. It was 'the dress'—remember? Was the dress white or blue? Could you see it both ways? This is a visual experiment in perception.

There is also an auditory version called the 'Yanny or Laurel' exercise. You are asked whether you hear the word Yanny or Laurel after hearing a recording of the word. Interestingly, which one you hear can come down to your age—well, the age of your ears.[54] The science behind it says that younger ears hear pitch differently. There are several links on YouTube to try it out, but this one is my favorite — https://www.youtube.com/watch?v=yDiXQl7grPQ.

Whether you do a visual or auditory experiment, the key is to get those that see or hear the opposite together and have them discuss why it is one or the other.

Exercises in empathy are a great way to engage everyone in a non-threatening manner and create some very grassroots ah-ha moments of enlightenment—and ultimately build a sense of understanding and belonging!

Stories of Origin

Another way to build a sense of belonging is to show genuine interest in others. It should begin with leaders. Take the time and tell your story from the board and C-Suite down. When you model openness, vulnerability, and uniqueness, it will open the

---

[54] https://www.theguardian.com/technology/2018/may/16/yanny-or-laurel-sound-illusion-sets-off-ear-splitting-arguments

door for others to share their stories. Managers and leaders should talk about the barriers they have faced, mistakes made—and, yes, success along the way.

It shouldn't be scripted or unauthentic. Fumbling through is to be authentic, which is what is needed. In the beginning, it may feel a little raw, but the point is to make connections and reduce people's fear of sharing their stories. A sense of belonging is built on trust, commonalities, and caring. What better way to get that ball rolling?

I will leave you with this:

- "If we want people to feel safe, then mistakes don't exist. We don't cast judgment making mistakes unpalatable.
- If we want people to feel love, then systems and behaviors have to put humans ahead of stuff.
- If we want people to feel whole, we must bring our whole selves to work, just as we are."[55]

REFLECTION AND APPLICATION

- Is the organization stuck in the diversity/equity loop?
- Do you have a culture of invitation or inclusion?
- Do you know whether your people have a sense of belonging?
- How do you continue to create and maintain a sense of belonging organically?

---

[55] https://www.teamawesomecoaching.com/moving-beyond-diversity-and-inclusion-to-belonging/

CHAPTER 11

INCLUSIVE LEADERSHIP

> *"Inclusive leadership is about leveraging differences to create a culture where everyone feels psychologically safe to contribute their unique perspectives, driving impactful outcomes and fostering organizational success."*
> – T. Renee' Smith

In This Chapter

- What is Inclusive Leadership?
- Why Inclusive Leadership Matters?
- The Signature Traits of Inclusive Leaders
- Reflection and Application

What is Inclusive Leadership

Leadership is about MORE than telling people what to do all the time.

Inclusive leadership isn't just a trendy term—it's a way of thinking and acting that transforms workplaces into vibrant, diverse communities where everyone feels valued and empowered. It's all about recognizing and celebrating the unique strengths and perspectives that each person brings to the team. Inclusive leaders create environments where differences aren't just accepted; they're embraced as vital ingredients for sparking innovation, creativity, and overall success.

Inclusive leadership isn't about telling people what to do all the time. It's about actively listening to diverse viewpoints, respecting different cultural backgrounds, and promoting fairness across the board. It's about making sure every team member feels like they belong, encouraging them to speak up without fear of being judged or left out. True inclusivity goes beyond surface-level differences like race or gender—it encompasses a wide range of experiences, skills, and outlooks that enrich the organization.

On the flip side, inclusive leadership isn't about token gestures or meeting diversity quotas just for show. It's not about merely tolerating differences without integrating them fully into the organizational fabric. And it definitely isn't about favoritism or perpetuating biases, whether consciously or not. Instead, it's a proactive effort to break down barriers, challenge stereotypes, and create equal opportunities based on merit and potential.

Ultimately, inclusive leadership is a journey of growth and continuous learning. It's about bridging divides, nurturing talent, and harnessing the diverse strengths of your team to drive excellence and innovation. When leaders embrace inclusivity, they don't just create a more harmonious workplace—they unlock their team's full potential to achieve extraordinary results.

Why Inclusive Leadership Matters

In today's fast-changing global landscape, inclusive leadership isn't just a nice-to-have—it's a game-changer for driving organizational success and making a positive impact in society. It's not only about doing the right thing morally but also strategically positioning organizations to thrive in diverse, interconnected markets. By actively embracing and leveraging differences, inclusive leaders create a culture where everyone feels valued, respected, and empowered to bring their unique perspectives and talents to the table.

Benefits and Impacts of Inclusive Leadership

- **Enhanced Retention:** When organizations foster inclusivity, they reduce turnover and cut down on the hefty costs of hiring and training new team members, which can add up to 30% to 150% of an employee's annual salary.

- **Improved Productivity:** Inclusive leaders cultivate an environment where team members feel safe to give their best. This boosts productivity because engaged employees are motivated to perform at their peak.

- **Increased Innovation:** Diversity in thoughts and experiences sparks creativity and innovation. Inclusive leaders harness diverse perspectives to develop fresh solutions and strategies that drive organizational growth and keep them competitive.

- **Enhanced Profits:** Companies with inclusive leadership practices tend to perform better financially. Research shows that those in the top quartile for ethnic and cultural diversity in management are 36% more likely to have higher profitability.

- **Reflective Workforce:** Inclusive leadership ensures that the organization's workforce mirrors the diversity of its customers and communities. This alignment helps in understanding and meeting the needs of diverse markets.

- **Better Decision-Making:** Inclusive leaders gather a wide range of viewpoints, leading to well-informed decisions. This inclusivity reduces the risks of groupthink and improves decision quality.

- **Improved Talent Acquisition:** Organizations known for their inclusive cultures attract top talent from diverse backgrounds. Inclusive leaders create environments where prospective employees see themselves thriving and contributing effectively.

- **Legal Compliance and Risk Mitigation:** Inclusive practices help organizations comply with diversity regulations, reducing legal risks related to discrimination and building a positive reputation.

- **Ethical and Social Responsibility:** Inclusive leaders prioritize fairness, equity, and ethical behavior, contributing positively to corporate social responsibility efforts and enhancing the organization's community reputation.

- **Employee Well-Being:** Inclusive workplaces support employee well-being by reducing stress and fostering a sense of belonging and support. This promotes better mental health and overall job satisfaction.

Inclusive leadership isn't just about doing the right thing—it's a strategic advantage that boosts organizational performance, fuels innovation, and ensures sustainable growth in today's diverse world.

The Signature Traits of Inclusive Leaders

Inclusive leaders embody six key traits that spell the difference between a thriving organization and one that falls short. These six standout traits define exceptional leaders—traits that not only align organizational and personal values but also foster collaboration across diverse perspectives. By embracing diversity in all its forms—whether it's different viewpoints, backgrounds, or experiences—these leaders create environments where every individual feels valued, respected, and empowered to bring their best to the table.

Leading inclusively isn't just a choice; it's a strategic advantage. When leaders champion diverse perspectives and experiences, they cultivate environments that spark creativity, drive innovation, and enhance team cohesion. These benefits ripple through the organization, strengthening decision-making and fostering a culture of unity and collaboration.

On a personal level, inclusive leaders experience profound growth and fulfillment. They forge deep connections with their teams, inspiring loyalty and commitment, and nurturing a sense of belonging that transcends organizational boundaries.

Conversely, the risks of neglecting inclusivity are substantial. Leaders who overlook diversity and inclusion risk perpetuating biased environments, eroding morale, and missing out on opportunities for growth and innovation. They may struggle to attract and retain top talent, lagging behind in a competitive global landscape.

Our proprietary **T.H.R.I.V.E. Framework for Inclusive Leadership** not only aligns values but also encourages collaboration across differences to achieve impactful outcomes. It's more than just a framework; it's a blueprint for leaders who aspire to build resilient, innovative, and inclusive organizations.

Signature Trait #1: Transparency and Accountability

In today's fast-paced workplaces, transparency and accountability aren't just catchy phrases—they're crucial elements of effective leadership. Transparent leaders prioritize openness in their actions and decisions, which builds trust and confidence among their teams. They understand that transparency goes beyond sharing information; it's about creating a culture where honesty and clarity prevail.

- **Strategic Decision-Making:** Inclusive leaders excel in strategic decision-making by involving their teams and considering diverse perspectives. They know that transparent decision-making builds consensus and commitment among team members, leading to stronger outcomes.

- **Being Open and Responsible in Actions and Decisions:** Transparency starts with leaders modeling openness and responsibility. They communicate clearly about their decisions, explain their rationale, and discuss how choices impact the organization. By being accountable, they set a standard that encourages accountability throughout the team.

- **Authenticity and Vulnerability:** Authentic leaders see vulnerability as a strength. They're genuine in their interactions, showing vulnerability when appropriate, which builds authentic connections and trust. This openness creates a supportive environment where team members feel safe to express themselves.

- **Creating a Culture of Trust and Psychological Safety:** Inclusive leaders prioritize fostering a culture of trust and psychological safety. They encourage open dialogue, welcome diverse viewpoints, and ensure team members feel valued and respected. This culture empowers individuals to speak up, share ideas, and take calculated risks without fear of backlash.

- **Fairness and Respect:** Fairness and respect are core values for inclusive leaders. They treat all team members equitably, ensuring decisions are based on merit and fairness rather than bias. By upholding these principles, they foster a culture of fairness and mutual respect across the organization.

- **Transparency in Processes and Communication:** Transparent leaders ensure processes and communication are clear, accessible, and consistent. They regularly update their teams on organizational developments, seek feedback, and openly discuss both challenges and successes. This transparency builds trust and alignment, ensuring everyone is informed and empowered to contribute effectively.

Transparency and accountability are vital traits of inclusive leadership that pave the way for organizational success. By practicing transparency in decision-making, fostering a trusting culture, and upholding fairness and respect, leaders not only strengthen their teams but also create environments where innovation thrives and individuals flourish. Transparent leaders inspire confidence, promote collaboration, and drive sustainable growth, making transparency a cornerstone of effective leadership in today's diverse and fast-paced world.

Signature Trait #2: Holistic Wellness

Inclusive leadership isn't just about hitting targets; it's about ensuring the overall well-being of both leaders and their teams.

Leaders who prioritize holistic wellness understand that personal well-being—mind, body, and spirit—is crucial for their effectiveness. They know that by setting an example with healthy habits and creating a supportive environment, they can boost team productivity and well-being.

- **Importance of Personal Well-Being for Leaders – Mind, Body, and Spirit**: Holistic wellness starts with leaders making their own well-being a priority. Whether it's getting enough sleep, eating healthily, exercising regularly, or practicing mindfulness, leaders show their teams the value of self-care and resilience.

- **Encouraging Work-Life Integration**: Inclusive leaders advocate for work-life integration, not just balance. They understand that seamlessly blending personal and professional lives leads to greater satisfaction and productivity. They support flexible work arrangements, respect personal boundaries, and promote time-management practices that honor both work responsibilities and personal well-being.

- **Promoting Mental Health Awareness**: Proactive inclusive leaders promote open discussions about mental health within their teams. They work to reduce stigma, provide resources for stress management, and build resilience. By fostering a culture that prioritizes mental well-being, they create an environment where team members feel supported and empowered.

- **Supporting Holistic Wellness Practices (Self-Care versus Self-Maintenance):** Leaders distinguish between self-care, which enhances holistic wellness, and mere self-maintenance, which meets basic needs. They encourage team members to prioritize practices that rejuvenate and restore, not just maintain productivity. This support helps build a workforce that's engaged, motivated, and resilient.

- **Effective Time-Management – Focusing on Outcomes and Not Just Effort:** Inclusive leaders stress effective time-management focused on outcomes rather than just effort. They empower their teams to set realistic goals, prioritize tasks, and manage workloads efficiently. This approach boosts efficiency and prevents burnout, ensuring sustainable productivity.

- **Overcoming Impostor Syndrome:** Inclusive leaders help their teams combat impostor syndrome by fostering a culture of acceptance and celebrating achievements. They promote self-reflection, offer constructive feedback, and challenge perfectionism. By nurturing self-confidence and resilience, they empower individuals to reach their full potential without doubts holding them back.

- **Preventing the Burn-Out Cycle:** Proactive inclusive leaders take steps to prevent burnout among their teams. They promote work-life balance, encourage breaks, and provide opportunities for rejuvenation. By recognizing signs of burnout early and addressing them, they ensure lasting performance and well-being within their teams.

Holistic wellness isn't just a personal choice; it's a strategic imperative for inclusive leaders. By prioritizing their own well-being, modeling healthy habits, and supporting holistic practices among their teams, leaders create environments where productivity, creativity, and engagement thrive. Holistic wellness builds resilience, prevents burnout, and enhances overall organizational performance, making it indispensable for inclusive leadership in today's fast-paced workplaces.

Signature Trait #3: Resilience and Flexibility

Inclusive leadership is all about being adaptable and resilient—qualities that help leaders navigate challenges, foster diversity, and drive positive change. Leaders who embody resilience and flexibility not only bounce back from setbacks but also embrace uncertainty and promote inclusivity through their actions.

- **Adapting to Change and Uncertainty:** Inclusive leaders excel in navigating change and uncertainty. They see change as an opportunity for growth, adjust their strategies swiftly, and inspire confidence in their teams during times of flux. By showing resilience, they encourage their teams to embrace change positively and innovate in response to challenges.

- **Bouncing Back from Setbacks:** Resilient leaders view setbacks as learning opportunities, not failures. They maintain a positive outlook, learn from setbacks, and motivate their teams to persevere through adversity. By modeling resilience, they nurture a culture of determination and resilience within their organizations.

- **Embracing Flexibility in Leadership Style:** Inclusive leaders understand the importance of flexibility in leadership. They adapt their approach to fit different situations and individuals, recognizing that diverse teams thrive under varied leadership styles. By being flexible, they empower their teams to succeed in dynamic environments and leverage their unique strengths.

- **Openness and Curiosity:** Inclusive leaders are open-minded and curious. They actively seek out new perspectives and ideas, listen attentively to diverse viewpoints, and value different opinions. By cultivating curiosity, they foster inclusivity and creativity within their teams.

- **Challenging the Status Quo:** Resilient leaders challenge norms and advocate for inclusivity and fairness. They address biases and inequities, initiate difficult conversations, and champion diversity in decision-making. By challenging the status quo, they create opportunities for positive change and cultivate a culture of inclusivity and belonging.

- **Speaking Up Against Bias:** Inclusive leaders courageously speak out against bias and discrimination, including their own biases. They reflect on their biases, acknowledge their impact, and take steps to address them. By modeling self-awareness and accountability, they create a safe environment where team members feel comfortable discussing biases openly. They advocate for equity, address microaggressions, and promote a culture of respect and fairness.

- **Taking Risks to Promote Inclusivity:** Resilient leaders take calculated risks to advance diversity and inclusion initiatives within their organizations. They support EDI-focused initiatives even in uncertain situations, driving meaningful change and demonstrating their commitment to creating inclusive workplaces.

- **Humility and Modesty:** Inclusive leaders practice humility by recognizing their limitations and valuing others' strengths. They seek feedback, admit mistakes, and learn from diverse perspectives. By fostering humility, they build trust and collaboration, empowering their teams to contribute authentically and innovate collectively.

- **Resourcefulness and Seeking Expertise When Needed:** Inclusive leaders demonstrate resourcefulness by leveraging available resources and seeking expert input when necessary. They cultivate diverse networks, tap into collective knowledge, and collaborate with experts to address complex challenges. By being resourceful, they enhance problem-solving capabilities and support inclusive decision-making processes.

Resilience and flexibility are essential to inclusive leadership. By adapting to change, embracing flexible leadership styles, challenging biases, and promoting inclusivity through courageous actions, leaders create environments where diversity thrives and innovation flourishes. These qualities inspire confidence, empower teams, and drive sustainable growth in today's rapidly evolving workplaces.

Signature Trait #4: Inclusive Communication and Collaboration

Being a great leader isn't just about giving orders—it's about connecting with your team in meaningful ways. Inclusive leaders get this. They know that effective communication isn't just about words; it's about listening with empathy, adapting to diverse audiences, and creating a space where everyone feels heard and respected.

- **Effective Communication Strategies:** Inclusive leaders communicate clearly and respectfully, ensuring that information flows smoothly across all levels of the organization. They adjust their style to fit different audiences, making sure their messages are understood and meaningful.

- **Empathetic Listening Skills:** They don't just hear—they listen. Inclusive leaders take the time to understand others' viewpoints without judgment. This builds trust and openness, making team members feel valued and appreciated.

- **Adaptive Communication Across Diverse Audiences:** Recognizing the diversity within their teams, inclusive leaders tailor their communication to connect with various cultural backgrounds, communication styles, and preferences. This approach fosters inclusivity and prevents misunderstandings.

- **Conflict Resolution Techniques:** Inclusive leaders handle conflicts by promoting **CARE-frontation**—a constructive approach focused on understanding and resolving issues. This method encourages mutual respect and healthy dialogue to find solutions together.

- **Utilizing Polarity Thinking:** Ever heard of polarity thinking? It's about balancing opposing forces—like short-term versus long-term goals or innovation versus tradition. Inclusive leaders use this approach to navigate complex challenges, finding solutions that blend different viewpoints and keep the team moving forward. Why does it matter? Because life isn't black and white; it's about finding harmony in the gray areas. Inclusive leaders use polarity thinking to foster creativity, resilience, and a workplace where everyone's voice matters.

- **Change Management:** They guide their teams through change by being open and transparent, addressing concerns, and involving team members in the process. Inclusive leaders understand how change affects individuals and teams, promoting resilience and adaptability.

- **Performance Coaching** - Inclusive leaders actively coach team members to enhance their personal and professional development. They provide constructive feedback, set clear goals, and support individuals in overcoming challenges. By identifying strengths and areas for improvement, inclusive leaders empower their team to increase productivity, achieve goals, and foster continuous growth.

- **Building High-Performance Teams:** Inclusive leaders cultivate high-performance teams by encouraging collaboration, leveraging diverse strengths, and empowering individuals to contribute their best work. This approach fuels innovation and achieves exceptional results.

- **Enhancing Team Cohesion:** Through inclusive communication and collaboration, leaders strengthen team bonds by creating a shared sense of purpose and belonging. Team members are motivated to work together towards common goals, boosting productivity and morale.

- **Fostering Collaboration and Teamwork:** They break down silos and foster cross-functional cooperation, maximizing the organization's collective potential. Inclusive leaders champion inclusivity, ensuring diverse perspectives shape decision-making, driving innovation, productivity, and organizational success.

Inclusive leaders know that effective communication and collaboration are the cornerstones of a workplace where every team member feels valued and empowered. They lead by example, creating an environment where diversity isn't just acknowledged—it's celebrated and integrated into every aspect of the organization's journey towards excellence.

Signature Trait #5: Values-Driven Leadership and Executive Presence

Inclusive leadership isn't just about managing teams—it's about leading with integrity, inspiring trust, and embodying values that guide both personal and organizational success. Values-driven leadership and executive presence are crucial traits that define exceptional leaders in today's dynamic workplaces.

- **Leading with Integrity and Ethical Decision-Making**: At the core of values-driven leadership is integrity. It's about consistently making decisions based on ethical principles and values. Inclusive leaders prioritize transparency and honesty in their actions, which fosters trust and accountability within their teams.

- **Aligning Personal Values with Organizational Goals**: Inclusive leaders understand the importance of aligning personal values with the goals and mission of the organization. They ensure that their decisions and actions reflect not only their own values but also those that resonate with the broader organizational culture. This alignment creates coherence and reinforces a shared sense of purpose among team members.

- **Developing Executive Presence and Influence:** Executive presence isn't just about appearance—it's about how leaders project confidence, authority, and credibility. Inclusive leaders enhance their executive presence by honing their communication skills, improving emotional intelligence, and cultivating a commanding presence that inspires and motivates others.

- **Confidence and Courage in Decision-Making:** Inclusive leaders exhibit confidence and courage when faced with tough decisions. They rely on their values and strategic vision to navigate uncertainties and challenges, inspiring confidence in their teams. Their decisive actions and willingness to take calculated risks demonstrate leadership strength and resilience.

- **Outcome-Driven Focus on Goals and Achievements:** A key trait of inclusive leaders is their focus on achieving tangible results. They set clear objectives, empower their teams to succeed, and hold themselves and others accountable for delivering outcomes. This commitment to measurable achievements fosters a culture of performance and continuous improvement.

- **Strategic and Visionary Leadership:** Strategic thinking and visionary leadership are pivotal for inclusive leaders. They anticipate trends, identify opportunities, and develop long-term strategies that position their organizations for success. By aligning their vision with inclusive practices, they pave the way for innovation and sustainable growth.

- **Servant Leadership:** Inclusive leaders embody servant leadership by prioritizing the needs of their team members above their own. They foster a supportive environment where everyone's contributions are valued, and they actively work to remove barriers that hinder team success. By serving others first, they build loyalty, trust, and a strong sense of community within their teams.

Values-driven leadership and executive presence are the bedrock of inclusive cultures where every team member thrives. By leading with unwavering integrity, aligning personal values seamlessly with organizational goals, and embodying bold decision-making prowess, inclusive leaders ignite a spark of inspiration within their teams. They cultivate environments where innovation flourishes, collaboration knows no bounds, and each individual's potential is fully realized. In these empowered spaces, diversity becomes a catalyst for extraordinary achievements, propelling organizations to unprecedented heights of success and influence.

Signature Trait #6: Emotional Savvy

Ever wondered what sets exceptional leaders apart in today's complex world? It's not just about IQ or technical prowess—it's about their emotional savvy. Imagine a leader who not only understands their own emotions but also navigates cultural nuances effortlessly. This is the essence of emotional savvy in inclusive leadership.

- **Emotional Intelligence and Cultural Intelligence**: Inclusive leaders excel in emotional intelligence (EI) and cultural intelligence (CQ). They understand the power of emotions in driving team dynamics and organizational culture. By mastering EI, they navigate interpersonal relationships with finesse, while CQ enables them to bridge cultural gaps and foster unity across diverse teams.

- **Self-Awareness and Emotional Regulation:** Emotional savvy starts with self-awareness—the ability to recognize one's own emotions and their impact. Inclusive leaders harness this awareness to regulate their emotions effectively, maintaining composure even in challenging situations. By modeling emotional regulation, they set a tone of resilience and stability within their teams.

- **Empathy and Compassion in Leadership:** Empathy is the cornerstone of emotional savvy. Inclusive leaders cultivate a deep understanding of others' perspectives and feelings, fostering a culture where every team member feels heard and valued. Their compassion extends beyond words to actionable support, creating a nurturing environment where individuals thrive personally and professionally.

- **Nurturing Inclusive Team Cultures:** Emotional savvy leaders actively nurture inclusive team cultures. They promote open communication, encourage collaboration, and celebrate diversity of thought. By valuing every team member's contributions, they create a sense of belonging that enhances team cohesion and performance.

- **Recognizing and Addressing Implicit Bias:** Inclusive leaders are vigilant about recognizing and addressing implicit biases within themselves and their organizations. They engage in continuous self-reflection and education to dismantle biases that can undermine inclusivity. By fostering awareness and accountability, they pave the way for fairer decision-making and a more equitable workplace.

- **Continuous Learner:** Emotional savvy leaders embrace lifelong learning. They seek opportunities to deepen their emotional intelligence, refine their cultural competence, and stay attuned to evolving social dynamics. This commitment to growth not only enriches their leadership but also inspires continuous improvement within their teams.

Inclusive leadership isn't just about skills—it's about emotional savvy that transforms organizational cultures. By mastering emotional intelligence, fostering empathy, and addressing biases head-on, inclusive leaders create environments where diversity thrives and innovation flourishes. They build teams that are not only high-performing but also resilient and united in their pursuit of excellence. Emotional savvy isn't just a trait—it's the heartbeat of inclusive leadership, driving meaningful impact and lasting success.

A Charge to All Leaders

Being an inclusive leader is a superpower that transforms workplaces and unlocks untapped potential. Imagine creating a space where every team member feels seen, heard, and valued, fueling a culture of innovation and collaboration. As a leader, you hold the key to unleashing your team's diverse talents and perspectives, driving trust and loyalty, and inspiring them to reach new heights. Embracing inclusivity means embracing a future where your team thrives amid change and challenges, growing stronger together.

Conversely, choosing not to lead inclusively can dim the potential within your team, leading to disengagement, stifled creativity, and missed opportunities. Without inclusivity, you risk higher turnover and increased conflicts, creating a stagnant work environment. The choice is yours: lead with empathy and openness, champion diverse perspectives, and cultivate a culture of continuous learning. By becoming an inclusive leader, you're not just shaping your team; you're pioneering a movement toward meaningful change and success.

REFLECTION AND APPLICATION

- How effectively am I currently fostering a culture of inclusivity within my team or organization?
- Reflecting on the signature traits of inclusive leadership discussed (e.g., values-driven leadership, emotional savvy), which traits resonate most with my leadership style? How can I enhance these traits to better support a diverse and inclusive workplace?
- What specific actions can I take in the coming weeks to strengthen my inclusive leadership skills? How can I incorporate these actions into my daily practices and interactions with my team members?

CHAPTER 12

UNPACKING PRIVILEGE: INSIGHTS FOR INCLUSIVE LEADERSHIP

> *"Privilege is often invisible to those who have it."*
> – Michael Kimmel

In This Chapter

- What is Privilege
- Misconceptions About Privilege
- Different Types of Privilege
- The Importance of Leaders Understanding Privilege
- Reflection and Application

What is Privilege - Understanding Privilege in Everyday Life

Privilege isn't always easy to spot. It's not just about wealth or status; it's about the advantages that shape our experiences and opportunities in subtle yet profound ways. From the neighborhoods we grow up in to the schools we attend, and even the way we navigate daily interactions, privilege influences how the world responds to us.

Imagine privilege as an invisible backpack we carry, filled with advantages that others might not have. It's not just about having more; it's about facing fewer obstacles because of who we are or how society perceives us. While we often hear about racial or economic privilege, there are countless other types that shape our lives in ways we might not even realize.

In this chapter, we'll explore the many dimensions of privilege—beyond race, gender and wealth—and delve into how recognizing and understanding these privileges can foster a more equitable and inclusive world. We'll look at privilege in terms of ability, education, and more, examining how each type influences our daily lives and interactions. By shedding light on these often-overlooked aspects, I aim to broaden our perspectives and encourage meaningful dialogue about creating a fairer society for all.

Recognizing Privilege in the Workplace

Privilege in the workplace extends beyond salary and job title—it encompasses a complex web of advantages that influence career trajectories, interactions with colleagues, and overall professional experiences. Often, it's not explicitly acknowledged or discussed, yet it profoundly shapes workplace dynamics and opportunities.

In the context of work, privilege can manifest in various forms. It might be evident in the ease with which someone networks and gains mentorship, or in the assumptions made about competence based on appearance or background. Privilege can affect who gets promoted, whose voice is heard in meetings, and even whose ideas are credited.

Understanding workplace privilege involves recognizing how factors like gender, race, socio-economic background, education, and even physical ability can impact one's career journey. It's about acknowledging the advantages some individuals have due to societal norms and biases, which can unconsciously favor certain groups over others.

Understanding privilege isn't about guilt or blame; it's about awareness and empathy.

In this chapter, we'll explore the nuances of privilege in the workplace and how it influences professional interactions, career progression, and organizational culture. By unpacking these dynamics, we aim to promote awareness, foster inclusivity, and encourage proactive efforts to level the playing field for all employees.

Common Misconceptions About Privilege

Misconceptions about privilege often cloud discussions on equity and fairness in society. These misunderstandings can hinder progress toward creating inclusive environments where everyone has equitable opportunities to thrive. By unraveling these misconceptions, we can better grasp the nuanced ways privilege operates and its impact on individuals, workplaces, and communities. This understanding is crucial for fostering empathy, promoting diversity, and dismantling systemic barriers that perpetuate inequity.

- **Misconception: Privilege means you didn't work hard.**
  - **Reality:** Privilege doesn't negate hard work. It acknowledges that some people face fewer obstacles or barriers due to factors like race, gender, or economic status. It's about recognizing that while hard work is essential, not everyone starts from the same place.
- **Misconception: I haven't experienced privilege, so it doesn't affect me.**
  - **Reality:** Privilege isn't always obvious or explicit. It can be subtle, such as assumptions made about your competence based on your appearance or how easily you navigate through daily life without barriers that others face.
- **Misconception: Talking about privilege is about blaming or feeling guilty.**
  - **Reality:** Acknowledging privilege is about understanding societal advantages and using that awareness to advocate for equity and fairness. It's not about blame but rather recognizing systemic advantages that contribute to disparities.
- **Misconception: Privilege is only about race or gender.**
  - **Reality:** Privilege comes in many forms, including socioeconomic status, education, physical ability, and

more. It's about recognizing that advantages can exist across various aspects of identity and social status.

- **Misconception: We're all equal, so privilege doesn't matter.**
  - **Reality:** While equity (not equality) is a goal, recognizing privilege helps us understand and address disparities in opportunities and outcomes. It's about striving for fairness and inclusivity by dismantling barriers that create unequitable starting points.

- **Misconception: Privilege means life is easy for you.**
  - **Reality:** Having privilege doesn't mean life is free from challenges or hardships. It means certain aspects of life may be easier due to societal advantages, but everyone faces personal struggles and obstacles regardless of privilege.

- **Misconception: Privilege is a personal attack on individuals.**
  - **Reality:** Discussing privilege is about understanding systemic advantages and disadvantages rather than blaming individuals. It's about recognizing patterns and structures that perpetuate inequity rather than assigning personal fault.

- **Misconception: Privilege is static and unchangeable.**
  - **Reality:** While privilege can provide ongoing advantages, societal changes and personal actions can impact privilege over time. Acknowledging privilege is a starting point for promoting fairness and equity through awareness and advocacy.

In challenging misconceptions about privilege, we open pathways to deeper understanding and meaningful change. By acknowledging the complexities of privilege and its pervasive influence, we can work towards creating a more just and equitable world where everyone's potential is recognized and nurtured. Embracing these insights empowers us to advocate for systemic changes that benefit all, paving the way for a future where privilege no longer dictates one's opportunities or outcomes.

Different Types of Privilege

Have you ever stopped to think about the different ways privilege shows up in our lives and workplaces? Sometimes it's glaringly obvious, like when someone gets a promotion because they're part of a well-connected network. Other times, it's more subtle—like the unspoken advantage of growing up in a stable, two-parent household that instills confidence and security. Recognizing these privileges isn't just about identifying what's easy to see; it's also about uncovering what's hidden beneath the surface.

Imagine navigating a workplace where certain colleagues seem to effortlessly climb the career ladder while others struggle despite equal or even greater effort. It's in these moments that privilege becomes a crucial lens through which we can understand disparities in opportunities and outcomes. Yet, many people remain oblivious to their own privilege, which can lead to misunderstanding and frustration when they encounter others who face barriers they've never had to confront.

Understanding different types of privilege isn't about guilt or blame; it's about awareness and empathy. It's about acknowledging the advantages we may take for granted and using that awareness to advocate for fairness and inclusivity. By unraveling the complexities of privilege, we can pave the way for a more equitable future where everyone has a chance to thrive based on their merit and potential.

In our diverse and interconnected world, privileges come in many forms, influencing everything from career opportunities and social interactions to personal well-being and access to resources. Let's explore different types of privilege:

Social and Cultural Privilege

- **White Privilege:** White privilege is having advantages and opportunities simply because society sees you as white
- **Male Privilege:** Advantages conferred to men in society, such as in career opportunities, pay equity, and social status
- **Heterosexual Privilege:** Benefits that heterosexual individuals experience in legal, social, and cultural settings
- **Cisgender Privilege:** Advantages experienced by individuals whose gender identity matches their sex assigned at birth
- **Christian Privilege:** Benefits and social advantages associated with being Christian in predominantly Christian societies
- **Language Privilege:** Advantages gained from fluency or proficiency in dominant languages within a society

Economic, Educational and Network Privilege

- **Class Privilege:** Socioeconomic advantages and access to resources based on financial status or social class
- **Financial Literacy Privilege:** Knowledge and skills related to managing finances and investments
- **Educational Privilege:** Opportunities and benefits gained from access to quality education and academic resources
- **Network Privilege:** Access to influential networks and connections that can provide opportunities for career advancement or support

Family and Community Privilege

- **Two-Parent Household Privilege:** Benefits and stability often associated with growing up in a household with two parents
- **First-Born Privilege:** Opportunities or expectations that come with being the eldest child in a family including receiving more attention and responsibility from parents, being seen as a role model for younger siblings, and having earlier access to privileges or opportunities within the family structure
- **Only Child Privilege** - Advantages experienced by individuals raised without siblings, such as receiving undivided parental attention, accessing more resources within the family, and developing independence early on
- **Parental Leave Privilege:** Benefits and support provided to individuals who have access to parental leave from work

Physical and Health Privilege

- **Thin Privilege:** Benefits attributed to individuals perceived as having a socially acceptable body weight or size
- **Beauty Privilege:** Assumptions made about an individual's competence, capabilities, and social status based on their physical appearance
- **Ability Privilege:** Advantages that non-disabled individuals experience in society, such as easier access to physical spaces, social interactions, and employment opportunities
- **Health Privilege:** Benefits and advantages associated with good health and access to healthcare

Citizenship, and Environmental Privilege

- **Citizenship Privilege:** Rights and benefits conferred to individuals based on their citizenship status in a particular country
- **Urban Privilege:** Access to resources, opportunities, and cultural amenities available in urban areas
- **Safe Neighborhood Privilege:** Benefits of living in a neighborhood or community with low crime rates and good public services

Understanding the spectrum of privileges, whether they're overt or subtle, is crucial for fostering empathy, equity, and inclusivity in our communities and workplaces. By acknowledging these advantages, we not only become more aware of our own positions but also more sensitive to the experiences of those who may not share the same privileges. It's a journey towards building fairer, more supportive environments where everyone has the opportunity to thrive based on their abilities and efforts, rather than on inherent advantages. Embracing this awareness can lead to meaningful changes that contribute to a more just and inclusive society overall.

The Importance of Leaders Understanding Privilege

Today's leaders are navigating teams that span multiple cultures, generations, and backgrounds. As leaders, understanding privilege is crucial in fostering an environment where everyone can thrive. Privilege influences how individuals perceive and experience the world, affecting opportunities, access to resources, and interactions within the team. By acknowledging and addressing privilege, leaders can create inclusive cultures that celebrate diversity and empower each team member to contribute fully. This understanding not only enhances team dynamics but also drives organizational success by leveraging the strengths of a diverse workforce.

Here's how understanding privilege impacts leaders:

- **Promoting Equity**: Leaders can actively work towards creating fair and inclusive environments by acknowledging and addressing privilege disparities
- **Effective Decision-Making**: Awareness of privilege helps leaders make informed decisions that consider the diverse

needs and perspectives of their team members and stakeholders

- **Building Trust**: Recognizing privilege fosters trust and credibility among team members who may come from different backgrounds or have varying levels of privilege
- **Enhancing Innovation**: Diverse perspectives, enabled by an understanding of privilege, can drive innovation and problem-solving within teams and organizations
- **Mitigating Bias**: Leaders can mitigate unconscious bias by understanding how privilege influences perceptions, opportunities, and interactions within the workplace
- **Empowering Leadership**: By addressing privilege, leaders can model behaviors that empower others to recognize and leverage their own privileges responsibly

I used to lead by example but it was too much work.

- **Fostering Inclusion**: Understanding privilege supports efforts to create inclusive cultures where all team members feel valued, respected, and heard

- **Achieving Organizational Goals**: Organizations that prioritize understanding privilege are more likely to attract and retain diverse talent, leading to improved performance and achievement of strategic objectives

Charge to Leaders

Privilege is like a lens through which we see the world, and recognizing it can open the door to positive change and greater understanding. As leaders, acknowledging privilege isn't about blame—it's an opportunity to foster empathy, awareness, and inclusivity. Imagine the impact you can have by using your position to create equitable opportunities and celebrate diverse voices. By understanding privilege, you can become a champion for fairness, leading a team where everyone feels valued and empowered to contribute their best.

Think of the ripple effect your leadership can create. Leaders who understand privilege are equipped to break down barriers, build trust, and inspire innovation. By appreciating diverse perspectives, you can make informed decisions that drive success and collaboration. Embrace the chance to turn privilege into a force for good, transforming your team into a dynamic and inclusive community. Your leadership can set the tone for an environment where every individual thrives, and together, you can achieve remarkable outcomes. The choice is yours, choose wisely.

REFLECTION AND APPLICATION

- Reflect on a time when you experienced privilege. How did it influence your opportunities and interactions?
- What are some misconceptions about privilege that you held before, and how have your views changed?
- How can you leverage your awareness of privilege to foster a more inclusive and equitable work environment?
- What specific actions can you implement to mitigate unconscious bias related to privilege in your leadership practices?
- How can you create opportunities for team members who may face barriers due to a lack of privilege?

CHAPTER 13

THE TRIAD OF SUCCESS: BUILDING A HIGH-PERFORMANCE CULTURE THROUGH MINDSET, SKILLSET, AND HEARTSET

> *"Culture eats strategy for breakfast."*
> – Peter Drucker

In This Chapter

- The Connection Between DEIB and a High-Performance Culture
- Myths about a High-Performance Culture
- What is a High-Performance Culture?
- What is a High Performance Team?

- The Pillars of a High-Performance Culture: Mindset, Skillset, and Heartset
- Practical Strategies for Implementing a High Performance Culture
- Reflection and Application

The Connection Between DEIB and a High-Performance Culture

DEIB isn't just a buzzword but a cornerstone for building a high-performance culture. It's easy to think of DEIB and high performance as separate entities—like DEIB is a nice-to-have and high performance is a must-have. But here's the truth: they're deeply intertwined, and together, they create a powerful synergy that drives organizational success.

First, think of DEIB as the foundation that supports a high-performance culture. When we talk about **diversity**, we're referring to having a mix of backgrounds, experiences, and perspectives within a team. This diversity brings different viewpoints and innovative ideas, which are essential for high performance. **Equity** ensures that everyone has the tools and opportunities they need to excel, leveling the playing field. **Inclusion** means everyone feels welcomed and valued, which boosts engagement and motivation. **Belonging** goes a step further, making sure everyone feels like they truly fit in and can be their authentic selves.

Now, how does this all play out in a high-performance culture? A high-performance culture thrives on clear goals, strong leadership, and a commitment to excellence. DEIB amplifies these elements by fostering a more inclusive environment where people are motivated to give their best. For instance, when employees see that their organization values diverse perspectives and provides equitable opportunities, they're more likely to be engaged and invested in their work. This increased engagement translates into higher productivity, better problem-solving, and more innovative solutions.

Moreover, a culture that embraces DEIB is often one where feedback is actively sought and valued, which is crucial for continuous improvement. When feedback flows freely in an inclusive environment, it leads to stronger team dynamics and more effective collaboration. This aligns perfectly with the goals of a high-performance culture, where ongoing growth and adaptability are key.

DEIB and high-performance culture aren't just compatible—they're complementary. By embedding DEIB into your organizational DNA, you're not only fostering a more inclusive and supportive workplace but also setting the stage for exceptional performance and success. By embracing the synergy between DEIB and high performance, you'll see your culture evolve into one that is thriving, innovative, and high-achieving.

Myths About a High Performance Culture

Myth 1: A high-performance culture is only about pushing employees to their limits.

- **Why It's a Myth:** This misconception suggests that high performance equates to overworking employees, often leading to burnout and decreased morale. In reality, a high-performance culture is about creating an environment where employees are motivated, supported, and engaged. It involves setting clear goals, providing necessary resources, and fostering a positive work environment that encourages employees to excel without sacrificing their well-being.

Example: Google's "20% Time" policy allows employees to spend 20% of their time on personal projects, fostering innovation and engagement while preventing burnout.

Myth 2: A high-performance culture is only about flashy perks and incentives.

- **Why It's a Myth:** While perks can enhance the work environment, they are not the core of a high-performance culture. True high-performance cultures focus on creating meaningful work, setting clear expectations, and providing support for personal and professional growth. Perks alone do not build a culture of excellence or drive sustained performance.

    Example: Salesforce, a leading cloud-based software company, is renowned for offering various perks like wellness programs and employee events, but its high-performance culture goes beyond these benefits. The company emphasizes a culture of trust, clear communication, and personal development. Salesforce invests heavily in leadership development programs and encourages a focus on values and purpose. It's the commitment to growth, clear goals, and a supportive work environment that truly drives their high performance, not just the external perks.

Myth 3: High-performance teams are only about having top talent.

- **Why It's a Myth:** While talent is important, a high-performance team is more than just a group of skilled individuals. It's about how well team members collaborate, communicate, and work together towards common goals. Team dynamics, trust, and shared purpose are crucial for high performance.

    Example: The success of the team behind NASA's Mars Rover missions illustrates that high performance comes from effective teamwork and collaboration, not just individual talent.

Myth 4: High-performance teams are created overnight.

- **Why It's a Myth:** Building a high-performance team is a process that requires time, effort, and ongoing development. It involves establishing trust, aligning goals, and continuously improving processes. Teams do not become high-performing instantly; it's the result of sustained effort and development.

    Example: The development of the high-performance team at Toyota involved years of commitment to continuous improvement and lean manufacturing practices.

Myth 5: High-performance cultures only benefit large organizations.

- **Why It's a Myth:** High-performance cultures are beneficial for organizations of all sizes. Small and mid-sized organizations can also create environments that drive excellence and engagement. It's not about the size of the organization but the commitment to creating a supportive and performance-oriented culture.

Example: Any organization can build a high-performance culture through a commitment to training, development, and employee empowerment.

We asked the employees for their feedback,
but after reprimanding those who spoke up, nobody else was forthcoming.

Myth 6: High-performance teams do not need regular feedback.

- **Why It's a Myth:** Regular feedback is essential for high-performance teams. It helps in identifying areas for improvement, reinforcing positive behaviors, and ensuring alignment with goals. Without ongoing feedback, teams may struggle with performance issues and lack direction. A continuous feedback loop of open communication without reprimand is vital in establishing trust and safety within the team.

Example: Despite its reputation for excellence and innovation, Microsoft places a strong emphasis on continuous feedback. The company implements regular feedback mechanisms such as performance reviews, peer evaluations, and real-time feedback tools to ensure that team members stay aligned with goals, adapt to new challenges, and continually improve. Microsoft's approach shows that even the highest-performing teams benefit greatly from ongoing feedback, which helps them refine their performance, stay motivated, and drive innovation.

Myth 7: A high-performance culture is just about having a great strategy.

- **Why It's a Myth:** While a solid strategy is important, a high-performance culture involves more than just strategic planning. It's about embedding values, fostering a supportive environment, and aligning daily practices with the organization's vision. Culture plays a crucial role in executing and sustaining strategic objectives.

    Example: Netflix's celebrated culture of freedom and responsibility goes hand-in-hand with its strategic objectives. Netflix's culture emphasizes autonomy and innovation, empowering employees to take risks and make decisions that align with the company's goals. This culture is deeply ingrained in the organization's DNA and supports its strategic vision of remaining a leader in the entertainment industry. By fostering a culture that values creativity and accountability, Netflix demonstrates that a high-performance culture is essential for executing and maintaining a successful strategy.

What is a High-Performance Culture?

A high-performance culture is one where the collective mindset, skillset, and heartset of a team drive success. It's not just about having the right strategy or resources; it's about creating an environment where everyone feels deeply connected to the organization's vision. In this kind of culture, employees don't just do their jobs—they're engaged and inspired by a shared sense of purpose that fuels their dedication and drive.

In a high-performance culture, collaboration and accountability are more than buzzwords—they're part of the daily routine. Team members work together seamlessly, share knowledge openly, and support each other's growth. There's a strong focus on continuous improvement, where feedback is welcomed and used to propel individuals and teams forward. This dynamic environment encourages innovation and problem-solving, making it a place where exceptional performance becomes the norm.

Ultimately, a high-performance culture creates a space where individuals are not only motivated to excel but also empowered to contribute their best. It's a culture where achievements are celebrated, and challenges are seen as opportunities for growth. By nurturing this kind of environment, organizations set themselves up for lasting success and a competitive edge in their industry.

What is a High-Performance Team?

A high-performance team is more than just a group of people working together—it's a well-oiled machine where every member plays a crucial role in driving toward a common goal. What sets these teams apart is their ability to leverage diverse skills and perspectives to not only meet expectations but consistently exceed them. They push boundaries and strive for excellence, always looking for ways to innovate and improve.

In a high-performance team, communication is crystal clear and happens regularly. Team members aren't just talking at each other; they're actively listening, sharing feedback, and collaborating in meaningful ways. Respect is a cornerstone of their interactions, and there's a deep appreciation for each individual's contributions. Everyone understands their role, knows how their work fits into the bigger picture, and is committed to both their own growth and the team's collective success.

These teams are driven by a shared vision and a passion for achieving more than what's expected. They celebrate their wins, learn from their challenges, and continuously look for ways to elevate their performance. By fostering a culture of collaboration, respect, and continuous improvement, high-performance teams set themselves up to achieve outstanding results and create a positive impact within their organization.

The Pillars of a High-Performance Culture: Mindset, Skillset, and Heartset

Creating a high-performance culture isn't just about hitting targets—it's about embedding the right mindset, skillset, and heartset into your organization. These pillars help foster an environment where everyone thrives and contributes to the organization's success.

Here's how each pillar plays a crucial role and how you can integrate DEIB principles into each one.

Mindset: The Foundation of a High-Performance Culture

Mindset is the cornerstone of a high-performance culture. It's about shaping how individuals think, feel, and approach their work. A positive, growth-oriented mindset helps teams align with the organization's vision, sets the stage for achieving ambitious goals, and drives continuous improvement. When everyone is on the same page about what's expected and why it matters, it creates a strong foundation for success. This alignment fuels motivation and commitment, making it easier to overcome challenges and exceed expectations.

- **Define Clear Goals and Expectations:** To build a high-performance culture, start by setting clear, measurable goals that align with your organization's vision. For example, you might set quarterly sales targets or customer satisfaction benchmarks. It's essential to communicate these goals effectively, ensuring everyone understands their role. Regular team meetings and straightforward written communications can help keep everyone on the same page. When setting performance expectations, aim for challenging yet attainable targets. For instance, a 10% increase in productivity can be motivating if you provide the necessary resources and support.

- **Establish Clear Metrics:** Tracking progress with clear metrics is vital. Define KPIs such as project completion rates or customer feedback scores to measure how well you're doing. For example, you might track the number of new clients acquired each quarter. Providing regular feedback is equally important. Schedule bi-weekly one-on-one meetings or performance reviews to reinforce positive behaviors and address any challenges that arise.

- **Cultivate Leadership Commitment:** Leaders play a critical role in fostering a high-performance culture. They should embody the values and behaviors they expect from their teams. For example, if innovation is a core value, leaders should actively participate in brainstorming sessions and support creative ideas. Their commitment to these values can inspire and motivate the entire organization.

Skillset: The Engine of High Performance

Skillset refers to the abilities and expertise that team members bring to the table. It's not just about having the right skills but also about continually developing and refining them. A robust skillset equips employees to tackle complex problems, adapt to changing demands, and drive innovation. Investing in training and development ensures that your team is not only capable but also prepared to push boundaries and deliver exceptional results. The right skillset transforms potential into performance, making it a critical component of a high-performance culture.

- **Empower and Develop Employees:** Empowering your team through development opportunities is key to high performance. Offer training programs and mentorship to help employees enhance their skills. This could include workshops on new technologies or leadership development programs. Recognize and reward high performance to keep motivation high, such as implementing an Employee of the Month award to celebrate achievements.

- **Training and Development:** A strategic approach to training is essential for maximizing your team's potential. Relying on employees to "pick things up as they go" places your organization at risk of financial loss, legal issues, and inefficiencies. Instead, provide targeted training that addresses specific skills required for their positions.

For example, if a role demands proficiency in compliance regulations, ensure employees receive comprehensive training on these regulations rather than leaving them to figure it out on their own. Continuous learning opportunities, such as online courses or industry conferences, should be provided to keep skills sharp and relevant. Utilize each team member's strengths to maximize performance. For instance, if someone excels in data analysis, involve them in projects that require these skills to leverage their expertise effectively.

- **Promote Collaboration and Teamwork:** A high-performance culture thrives on collaboration. Create an environment that encourages team projects and cross-departmental work. Regular team-building activities can help strengthen relationships and foster a collaborative spirit. When team members work together and respect diverse perspectives, the collective performance improves.

<u>Heartset: The Driving Force Behind Team Dynamics</u>

Heartset encompasses the emotional and relational aspects of a high-performance team. It's about creating a work environment where team members feel valued, supported, and connected to a shared purpose. A strong heartset fosters trust, encourages open communication, and drives a culture of feedback and continuous improvement. When individuals feel emotionally invested and recognized, they are more likely to contribute their best and support one another. This emotional alignment helps build resilience, drive innovation, and sustain high performance over time.

- **Create a Feedback-Rich Culture:** Building a culture of openness starts with feedback. Implement mechanisms like 360-degree feedback and regular performance reviews to gather input from all levels. Use surveys to collect feedback and address any issues that arise. Provide constructive feedback focusing on strengths and areas for improvement. For instance, after completing a project, discuss what went well and what could be improved to continually refine and enhance team performance.

- **Drive Innovation and Adaptability:** Encourage a culture of innovation by supporting creativity and risk-taking. Set up an "innovation lab" where employees can test new ideas without fear of failure. Promote adaptability by staying responsive to market changes and customer needs. For example, if customer feedback indicates a desire for new features, pivot quickly to address those needs and stay ahead of the competition.

- **Measure and Celebrate Success:** Establish KPIs to track progress toward goals, such as sales targets or project milestones. Regularly review these metrics and adjust strategies as needed to stay on track. Celebrate achievements to reinforce a culture of success. Team celebrations or public recognition of accomplishments can boost morale and motivate everyone to strive for continued success.

- **Promote Accountability and Performance:** Set clear expectations and performance metrics to ensure everyone knows what's required. For instance, establish monthly goals for project deliverables and review progress regularly. Ensure feedback is a continuous process by using tools like performance dashboards to provide real-time updates on progress, helping teams stay accountable and focused on their objectives.

Practical Strategies for Implementing a High-Performance Culture

Building a high-performance culture that integrates DEIB effectively involves more than just setting goals; it requires actionable strategies that make DEIB an integral part of your organization's daily operations. Here are some practical strategies to implement:

#1 - Create Inclusive Policies

- **Develop and Implement DEIB-Friendly Policies:** Start by crafting policies that explicitly support diversity, equity, inclusion, and belonging within the high-performance framework. This includes updating recruitment practices to ensure a diverse candidate pool, implementing flexible work arrangements to accommodate different needs, and establishing clear anti-discrimination policies. For example, create a policy that ensures equitable access to professional development opportunities for all employees, regardless of their background.

- **Ensure Policy Alignment:** Make sure these policies align with your organization's overall goals and performance standards. Communicate these policies clearly across the organization and integrate them into the company's values and mission. Regularly review and update policies to reflect the evolving needs of your workforce and industry best practices.

#2 - Foster Leadership Commitment

- **Lead by Example:** Leadership commitment is crucial for embedding DEIB into the organizational culture. Leaders should actively model the behaviors and values they want to see, such as participating in DEIB training and engaging in inclusive decision-making. For example, a senior leader could regularly share their own experiences with DEIB and highlight how these efforts contribute to team performance and success.

- **Support DEIB Initiatives:** Leaders should also champion DEIB initiatives by allocating resources, endorsing training programs, and setting clear expectations for all levels of management. This could involve hosting workshops on unconscious bias, establishing mentorship programs for underrepresented groups, or setting diversity goals for teams.

#3 - Inclusive Benefits

I have an employee on the line asking about inclusive benefits, but I'm not trained on what those are!

- **Offer Inclusive Benefits:** Design and implement employee benefits that cater to a diverse range of needs. This can include offering mental health resources, family leave policies, and financial support for various life stages and personal circumstances. For instance, provide flexible benefits packages that allow employees to choose options that best suit their individual needs, such as childcare support or wellness programs.

- **Communicate Benefits Clearly**: Ensure that all employees are aware of and understand the inclusive benefits available to them. Regularly update and promote these benefits to reflect changes in employee needs and industry trends.

- **Train Your Team on Benefits**: Make sure your team is well-trained on the benefits offered and how these benefits impact employees. Provide clear information and training sessions to help employees fully understand and utilize the available resources, ensuring they can make informed decisions about their benefits.

#4 - Engage Employees in DEIB Initiatives

- **Promote Active Participation**: Encourage employees to take an active role in DEIB initiatives by creating opportunities for them to contribute ideas and feedback. This might include forming DEIB committees, organizing focus groups, or hosting brainstorming sessions where employees can voice their thoughts on how to improve inclusivity and performance.

- **Measure Effectiveness:** Regularly assess the effectiveness of DEIB initiatives by gathering employee feedback through surveys, focus groups, or one-on-one conversations. Use this data to make informed adjustments and ensure that DEIB efforts are meeting the needs of your workforce. For example, if a survey reveals that employees feel underrepresented in decision-making processes, take steps to increase their involvement.

5 - Integrate DEIB into Performance Metrics

- **Set DEIB-Related Performance Goals:** Incorporate DEIB objectives into performance metrics to align them with the organization's high-performance standards. This could involve setting goals for increasing diversity within leadership roles, improving employee satisfaction scores related to inclusion, or measuring the impact of DEIB training on team dynamics.

- **Monitor and Adjust**: Regularly review performance data to track progress toward DEIB goals. Adjust strategies and initiatives based on these insights to ensure continuous improvement. For example, if data shows that certain DEIB training programs are particularly effective, consider expanding them to reach more employees.

#6- Build an Inclusive Environment

- **Create Brave and Safe Spaces for Dialogue:** Establish forums or safe spaces where employees can discuss DEIB topics openly. This can help build trust and encourage honest conversations about challenges and opportunities related to inclusivity. For instance, hosting monthly "DEIB dialogues" can provide a platform for employees to share their experiences and suggest improvements.

- **Recognize and Celebrate Diversity**: Celebrate the diverse backgrounds and achievements of your employees. This can be done through events, cultural awareness programs, or recognition initiatives that highlight contributions from diverse team members. For example, hosting an annual diversity day to recognize the various cultural backgrounds of your employees can foster a sense of belonging and pride.

#7 - Develop Inclusive Leadership Programs

- **Invest in DEIB Training for Leaders**: Provide specialized DEIB training programs for leaders to equip them with the skills and knowledge needed to drive inclusivity. This training can focus on areas such as understanding unconscious bias, managing diverse teams, and fostering an inclusive environment. For example, a leadership workshop might include role-playing scenarios that challenge leaders to navigate complex DEIB issues.

- **Create DEIB Leadership Accountability**: Establish accountability mechanisms where leaders are evaluated based on their commitment to DEIB. This could involve including DEIB-related objectives in performance reviews, setting clear targets for diversity in their teams, and requiring regular reporting on DEIB progress. For instance, leaders might be assessed on their efforts to mentor diverse talent and support inclusive initiatives.

#8 - Implement Inclusive Recruitment and Retention Practices

- **Revise Recruitment Strategies:** Ensure that your recruitment practices are designed to attract diverse candidates. This can involve using diverse job boards, partnering with organizations that support underrepresented groups, and implementing blind recruitment techniques to reduce bias. For example, include diverse interview panels and ensure job descriptions use inclusive language to appeal to a broader range of applicants.

- **Focus on Retention:** Develop retention strategies that support a diverse workforce, such as creating employee resource groups (ERGs) or mentorship programs tailored to underrepresented groups. Regularly check in with employees to understand their experiences and address any barriers to their advancement. For example, establishing an ERG for women in leadership can provide networking opportunities and support career growth.

#9 - Foster a Culture of Continuous Learning

- **Encourage Lifelong Learning:** Promote a culture where continuous learning is valued and supported. Offer access to DEIB-related learning resources, such as online courses, webinars, and industry conferences. Encourage employees to pursue personal development opportunities that enhance their understanding of inclusivity and high performance.

- **Create Knowledge-Sharing Platforms**: Establish platforms where employees can share their learning and insights on DEIB. This could be an internal blog, a knowledge-sharing session, or a community of practice focused on DEIB topics. For example, set up a monthly "DEIB Insights" meeting where employees present on recent learnings or best practices related to inclusivity.

#10 - Promote Transparent Communication

- **Share DEIB Goals and Progress:** Be transparent about your DEIB goals, strategies, and progress. Regularly update employees on the organization's DEIB efforts and share successes as well as areas for improvement. This openness can help build trust and ensure everyone is aligned with the organization's DEIB objectives.

- **Encourage Open Dialogue:** Create channels for open dialogue where employees can express their concerns and suggestions regarding DEIB. This might include anonymous feedback tools, open forums, or regular Q&A sessions with leadership. For example, implement an anonymous suggestion box where employees can submit ideas for enhancing inclusivity.

#11 - Integrate DEIB into Organizational Processes

- **Incorporate DEIB in Performance Reviews:** Ensure that DEIB principles are embedded in performance review processes. Include criteria related to inclusive behaviors, such as collaboration, respect for diversity, and support for DEIB initiatives. For example, performance reviews might assess how employees contribute to creating an inclusive team environment.

- **Embed DEIB in Organizational Policies:** Review and revise existing policies to ensure they support DEIB principles. This can include updating codes of conduct, revising compensation policies to ensure equity, and integrating DEIB considerations into decision-making processes. For instance, create a policy that mandates diversity in project teams to ensure varied perspectives are represented.

The choice is yours: you can build a culture where employees merely show up to get paid, or you can create an environment where they feel deeply connected, valued, and engaged.

Think about the difference. In a disconnected culture, people are just going through the motions. They might complete their tasks, but there's little passion or commitment. Employees clock in and out, focusing only on their paychecks and not on the bigger picture. This type of culture may get the job done, but it falls short in fostering innovation, loyalty, and high performance.

Now, imagine a workplace where every team member feels a genuine sense of belonging and appreciation. Here, people aren't just fulfilling their roles; they are thriving, driven by a shared purpose and an environment that nurtures their growth. This high-performance culture isn't just about meeting goals—it's about exceeding them through collaboration, creativity, and mutual respect. It's where DEIB principles aren't just policies but integral to how the organization operates, making every individual feel like a crucial part of the team.

In this thriving culture, employees are not only motivated but also inspired. They bring their best selves to work every day, contributing to a dynamic and successful organization. It's a culture where innovation flourishes, loyalty is strong, and performance reaches new heights.

As you reflect on the culture you want to create, ask yourself: Will you settle for a workplace where people are just going through the motions, or will you strive for an environment where they are fully engaged and empowered? The path to a high-performance culture is clear—choose to cultivate a workplace where everyone feels connected, valued, and motivated to excel. The impact on your organization will be profound and lasting.

REFLECTION AND APPLICATION

- What specific changes can we make to our policies and practices to better support DEIB and enhance our high-performance culture?

- How can we better communicate our goals and expectations to ensure that every team member understands and is aligned with our vision?

- What initiatives can we implement to regularly gather feedback and measure the effectiveness of our DEIB and high-performance efforts?

- How can we create more opportunities for employees to develop their skills and contribute meaningfully to our goals?

- What steps can we take to ensure that our leadership team consistently models the values and behaviors we want to see throughout the organization?

CHAPTER 14

IGNITING PASSION: THE POWER OF EMPLOYEE ENGAGEMENT

> *"Employee engagement is the emotional commitment the employee has to the organization and its goals."*
> – Kevin Kruse

In This Chapter

- Defining Employee Engagement: What It Means and Why It Matters
- Debunking the Myths About Employee Engagement
- The Impact of Employee Engagement: Fueling Success
- Key Metrics for Measuring Employee Engagement
- Strategies for Enhancing Employee Engagement
- Overlooked Aspects of Employee Engagement

- Developing an Action Plan
- Fostering Employee Engagement for Organizational Success
- Reflection and Application

Employee engagement isn't just about having happy employees; it's about having employees who are emotionally invested in their work and aligned with the organization's mission. When employees are engaged, they go beyond their job descriptions—they contribute ideas, they collaborate effectively, and they take pride in their work. This chapter explores what employee engagement truly means, its profound impact on organizational success, and dispels common misconceptions about it.

Defining Employee Engagement: What It Means and Why It Matters

- **Emotional Commitment and Alignment:** Employee engagement goes beyond mere job satisfaction. It reflects the emotional commitment employees have towards their work, their team, and the organization's goals. Engaged employees are passionate about their work and motivated to contribute to the organization's success. They align their personal values with the organization's mission, fostering a sense of purpose and fulfillment.

- **Intrinsic Motivation and Performance:** Engaged employees are driven by intrinsic motivation. They find meaning and satisfaction in their roles, which leads to higher productivity, creativity, and innovation. Unlike extrinsically motivated employees who are motivated by external rewards, engaged employees are self-motivated to excel and contribute positively to the organization's growth.

- **Two-Way Relationship:** Employee engagement is a mutual relationship between the organization and its employees. It requires proactive efforts from both sides—organizations must create a conducive environment that nurtures engagement, while employees must actively participate and contribute to the organizational goals. It's about fostering a culture where mutual trust, respect, and open communication thrive.

The Link Between Engagement and Organizational Success

- **Increased Productivity and Performance** - Engaged employees are more productive and perform at higher levels compared to their disengaged counterparts. They are committed to achieving organizational goals and are willing to go the extra mile to deliver results. This heightened performance directly contributes to the organization's overall success and competitiveness in the market.

- **Enhanced Innovation and Creativity** - Engagement fosters a culture where employees feel safe to share their ideas and perspectives. This environment promotes innovation and creativity as diverse viewpoints contribute to problem-solving and decision-making processes. Engaged employees are more likely to innovate and adapt to changing circumstances, driving continuous improvement within the organization.

- **Improved Customer Satisfaction** - Engaged employees provide better customer service and build stronger relationships with clients. Their enthusiasm and commitment translate into positive interactions with customers, leading to increased satisfaction, loyalty, and retention. Satisfied customers, in turn, contribute to the organization's reputation and long-term success.

Misconceptions and Realities: Understanding What Employee Engagement Is Not

- **Job Satisfaction vs. Engagement** - Employee engagement is often misconstrued as synonymous with job satisfaction. While job satisfaction is important, it primarily reflects an employee's contentment with their job conditions and benefits. Engagement, on the other hand, encompasses emotional commitment and active participation in achieving organizational goals, beyond mere satisfaction.

- **Engagement vs. Happiness** - Happiness at work is a transient state influenced by various factors, including personal circumstances and job satisfaction. Engagement, however, is a deeper connection that involves emotional investment, alignment with organizational values, and a sense of purpose. Engaged employees may not always be happy in every moment, but they are committed and motivated to contribute positively to the organization.

- **Measurement vs. Impact** - Employee engagement is often measured through surveys and metrics, but its true impact extends beyond numbers. It influences organizational culture, employee morale, and overall performance. Effective engagement strategies focus not only on measuring engagement levels but also on creating meaningful experiences that nurture a positive and productive work environment.

Employee engagement is the cornerstone of organizational success in today's competitive landscape. It goes beyond superficial measures of satisfaction or happiness—it's about creating a workplace where employees thrive, innovate, and contribute their best. By understanding what engagement truly entails, its profound impact on productivity, innovation, and customer satisfaction becomes clear. In the following sections, we'll explore key strategies for enhancing engagement, measuring its effectiveness, and creating a culture where engagement flourishes.

Debunking Myths About Employee Engagement

> *"Engagement is not something you can buy, it's something you must build—one meaningful interaction at a time."*
> – T. Rneee' Smith

Employee engagement is often misunderstood and surrounded by myths that can hinder efforts to create a thriving workplace culture. Let's unpack some of these myths to uncover the truth behind what really drives engagement.

Myth 1: Employee Engagement is Just About Happiness

- **Reality:** Employee engagement goes beyond happiness. While happy employees are more likely to be engaged, true engagement involves a deep emotional connection to the work and the organization. It's about commitment, motivation, and feeling valued.

Myth 2: Engagement is Solely HR's Responsibility

- **Reality:** Engaging employees is a collective effort that starts from top leadership down to every manager. It's about creating a culture where everyone feels involved, respected, and heard.

Myth 3: Engagement Means Perks and Benefits

- **Reality:** While perks and benefits can enhance employee satisfaction, true engagement is rooted in meaningful work, clear goals, and opportunities for growth. Engagement is about feeling challenged and recognized, not just receiving perks.

Myth 4: Engagement Can't Be Improved in Tough Times

- **Reality:** In challenging times, engagement becomes even more critical. Clear communication, empathy, and support can strengthen engagement and foster resilience among employees.

Myth 5: Engagement Is the Same for Everyone

- **Reality:** Engagement isn't one-size-fits-all. What gets one person excited about their work might not do the same for someone else. Successful engagement strategies understand and honor the diversity in how people work, what drives them, and what keeps them committed. Leaders who personalize their approach to match the individual needs of their team members build stronger and more enduring engagement.

Myth: Engagement is Measured by Employee Satisfaction Surveys Alone

- **Reality:** While surveys are useful, they only capture a snapshot of engagement. True engagement is shown in daily interactions, productivity, innovation, and the overall commitment employees show to their work.

By understanding and debunking these myths, organizations can refocus their efforts on what truly drives engagement: meaningful work, supportive leadership, and a culture that values every individual's contribution.

The Impact of Employee Engagement: Fueling Success

> *"Engaged employees are more productive, more profitable, more customer-focused, and more likely to stay."*
> *– Gallup*

Employee engagement isn't just a buzzword—it's a critical factor that directly influences organizational success. Engaged employees are not only committed to their work but also drive productivity, innovation, profitability, and customer satisfaction. This section explores the profound impact of employee engagement across various facets of organizational performance and success.

Increased Productivity: How Engaged Employees Drive Performance

- **Motivation and Commitment** - Engaged employees are motivated by more than just external rewards; they are driven by intrinsic factors like purpose and alignment with organizational goals. This intrinsic motivation translates into higher levels of productivity as employees go above and beyond to achieve their objectives.

- **Efficiency and Effectiveness** - Engaged employees are focused and efficient in their work. They prioritize tasks effectively, collaborate proactively with team members, and demonstrate a strong work ethic. This heightened efficiency leads to improved performance metrics and overall organizational success.

- **Quality of Work** - Employee engagement correlates with higher quality work output. Engaged employees are meticulous in their approach, paying attention to detail and striving for excellence in their deliverables. This commitment to quality enhances the organization's reputation and customer satisfaction.

Innovation and Creativity: Why Engagement Fosters New Ideas

- **Open Communication and Idea Generation** - Engaged employees feel empowered to share their ideas and perspectives without fear of criticism. This open communication fosters a culture of innovation where diverse viewpoints contribute to creative problem-solving and the development of innovative solutions.

- **Risk-Taking and Experimentation** - Engaged employees are more willing to take calculated risks and experiment with new approaches. They are innovative in their thinking, exploring alternative methods and embracing change to drive continuous improvement within the organization.

- **Adaptability to Change** - Engagement cultivates a mindset of adaptability and resilience. Engaged employees are receptive to change initiatives and actively participate in adapting to new challenges and opportunities. This agility enables the organization to stay competitive in dynamic market environments.

Profitability: The Financial Benefits of Engaged Teams

- **Cost Savings and Efficiency Gains** - Engaged teams contribute to cost savings through improved productivity, reduced absenteeism, and lower turnover rates. These efficiency gains translate into direct financial benefits for the organization, enhancing profitability and sustainability.

- **Revenue Growth and Customer Loyalty** - Engaged employees deliver exceptional customer service and build strong relationships with clients. Satisfied customers are more likely to remain loyal and advocate for the organization, driving revenue growth and enhancing long-term profitability.

- **Market Competitiveness** - Organizations with highly engaged teams are more competitive in the market. They attract top talent, innovate faster, and deliver superior products and services that meet customer expectations. This competitive advantage leads to sustainable growth and market leadership.

Employee Retention: Reducing Turnover Through Engagement

- **Job Satisfaction and Fulfillment** - Engaged employees experience higher job satisfaction and fulfillment in their roles. They feel valued and appreciated, which reduces the likelihood of seeking employment elsewhere. This retention of talent stabilizes the workforce and minimizes recruitment costs.

- **Career Development and Growth** - Engagement fosters a supportive environment where employees are encouraged to develop their skills and pursue career advancement opportunities. Organizations that invest in employee growth and development cultivate loyalty and long-term commitment.

- **Organizational Culture** - A culture of engagement promotes a sense of belonging and camaraderie among team members. Employees feel connected to the organization's mission and values, reinforcing their commitment to staying and contributing to its success.

Customer Satisfaction: The Connection Between Engaged Employees and Satisfied Customers

- **Service Excellence** - Engaged employees are passionate about delivering excellent customer service. They understand customer needs, anticipate preferences, and go the extra mile to exceed expectations. This dedication to service excellence enhances customer satisfaction and loyalty.

- **Brand Advocacy and Reputation** - Satisfied customers become advocates for the brand, promoting its products and services through word-of-mouth and positive reviews. Engaged employees play a crucial role in shaping the organization's reputation and building long-term relationships with customers.

- **Feedback Loop** - Engagement creates a feedback loop where satisfied customers provide valuable insights and recommendations. Engaged employees are receptive to customer feedback, using it to improve processes, products, and service delivery, thereby enhancing overall customer satisfaction.

Employee engagement is not just a beneficial attribute—it's a fundamental driver of organizational success. From boosting productivity and innovation to increasing profitability and customer satisfaction, the impact of engaged employees extends across every aspect of the organization. By fostering a culture of engagement and investing in employee well-being, organizations can unlock the full potential of their teams and achieve sustainable growth in today's competitive landscape.

Key Metrics for Measuring Employee Engagement

> *"Measuring engagement isn't just about numbers; it's about understanding the heartbeat of your organization."*
> *– T. Renee' Smith*

Measuring engagement isn't just about numbers; it's about understanding the heartbeat of your organization. Employee engagement metrics provide crucial insights into the health of your workforce. Beyond traditional satisfaction surveys, modern metrics offer a deeper understanding of what drives motivation, commitment, and performance among your employees. Let's explore how these metrics can illuminate the path towards a more engaged and productive workplace.

- **Traditional vs. Modern Metrics: Beyond Satisfaction Surveys**
    - *Traditional Metrics:* Annual or bi-annual employee satisfaction surveys have long been a staple in gauging overall employee happiness and job satisfaction. These surveys typically provide a snapshot of how employees feel about their roles, colleagues, and the organization as a whole. While they offer valuable insights, they often lack immediacy and may not capture evolving sentiments over time.
    - *Modern Metrics:* Real-time feedback tools, pulse surveys, and sentiment analysis have revolutionized how

organizations track employee engagement. These tools provide instant feedback on employee mood, satisfaction levels with specific projects or initiatives, and their overall sense of well-being at work. By capturing real-time data, organizations can respond swiftly to issues and proactively address concerns before they escalate.

- **Leading Indicators: Early Signs of Engagement**
    - ***Employee Participation:*** Participation rates in voluntary events or activities such as training sessions, workshops, and social gatherings serve as leading indicators of employee engagement. High participation rates often indicate a motivated workforce that values professional development and camaraderie. Leaders can use this metric to gauge interest in organizational initiatives and the overall enthusiasm of their teams.
    - ***Initiative and Contribution:*** The frequency and quality of employee suggestions, contributions, and innovative ideas are critical indicators of engagement. When employees actively contribute ideas, it demonstrates their commitment to improving processes, solving problems, and driving innovation within the organization. Leaders who track this metric can identify emerging leaders, foster a culture of continuous improvement, and harness the collective creativity of their teams.

- **Lagging Indicators: Long-term Impact on Performance and Retention**

    o *Performance Metrics:* Employee performance ratings, goal attainment, and skill development are essential lagging indicators of engagement. High-performing employees who consistently meet or exceed goals are often more engaged and motivated in their roles. By tracking performance metrics, organizations can identify top performers, provide targeted development opportunities, and align individual goals with organizational objectives.

    o *Retention Rates:* Turnover rates and reasons for employee departures provide valuable insights into the effectiveness of engagement initiatives. High turnover rates can indicate dissatisfaction, burnout, or a lack of alignment with organizational values. Conducting exit interviews and analyzing retention data helps leaders understand why employees leave and identify areas for improvement in workplace culture, leadership practices, or career development opportunities.

Effective employee engagement measurement goes beyond simple metrics; it's about capturing the pulse of your organization in real time. By utilizing a blend of traditional and modern metrics, leaders can gain a comprehensive view of employee sentiment, motivation, and commitment. These insights not only guide strategic decisions but also empower organizations to cultivate a culture where employees thrive and contribute their best.

Strategies for Enhancing Employee Engagement

> *"People may take a job for more money, but they often leave it for more recognition, responsibility, and opportunities for growth."*
> – T. Renee' Smith

Employee engagement isn't just about perks or benefits; it's about creating an environment where employees feel valued, motivated, and eager to contribute. When organizations invest in strategies that enhance engagement, they not only boost productivity but also cultivate a culture of loyalty and innovation. Let's explore practical ways leaders can enhance employee engagement across various dimensions.

- **Creating a Culture of Trust and Open Communication: Building Bridges of Connection** - Trust and Open Communication: Building trust through transparent communication and active listening fosters an environment where employees feel safe to share ideas, voice concerns, and collaborate effectively. When trust is established, it forms the foundation for a resilient and engaged workforce.

- **Empowering Employees: Opportunities for Growth and Development** - Growth and Development: Providing opportunities for skill development, career advancement, and personal growth empowers employees to take ownership of their professional journey. When employees see a path for growth within the organization, they are more likely to stay engaged and committed.

- **Recognition and Reward Programs: Beyond Monetary Incentives** - Meaningful Recognition: Recognizing and appreciating employees' efforts and achievements goes beyond monetary rewards. Personalized recognition, public acknowledgments, and tangible rewards tailored to individual preferences reinforce positive behaviors and motivate continued excellence.

- **Work-Life Balance: Supporting Well-being and Engagement** - Well-being and Balance: Supporting work-life balance initiatives, such as flexible work arrangements, wellness programs, and mental health resources, demonstrates organizational commitment to employee well-being. When employees feel supported in managing their personal and professional lives, they are more engaged and productive.

- **Diversity and Inclusion: Ensuring All Voices Are Heard** - Inclusive Environment: Fostering a culture of diversity and inclusion where every voice is heard and valued enhances engagement. Embracing diverse perspectives and creating opportunities for all employees to contribute promotes innovation, creativity, and a sense of belonging.

- **Leadership's Role in Driving Engagement: Leading by Example and Inspiring Others** - Inspirational Leadership: Leaders who lead by example, embodying the organization's values and demonstrating commitment to employee well-being and success, inspire trust and loyalty. Their vision, authenticity, and ability to motivate others are critical in driving employee engagement and organizational success.

Enhancing employee engagement requires a multifaceted approach that addresses both tangible and intangible aspects of workplace culture. By prioritizing trust, empowerment, recognition, work-life balance, diversity, inclusion, and inspirational leadership, organizations can create environments where employees thrive and contribute their best. These strategies not only boost morale and retention but also foster a dynamic and innovative workforce ready to tackle challenges and achieve collective goals.

Overlooked Aspects of Employee Engagement

> *"Employees who believe that management is concerned about them as a whole person—not just an employee—are more productive, more satisfied, more fulfilled. Satisfied employees mean satisfied customers, which leads to profitability."*
> *– Anne M. Mulcahy*

Employee engagement isn't just about surveys and perks; it's about creating a workplace where people feel connected, valued, and inspired. Let's explore some often-overlooked aspects that are essential for fostering a deeply engaged workforce:

- **Emotional Engagement: Connecting Employees to the Organization's Mission** - It's more than just a job; it's about aligning personal values with what the organization stands for. When employees see how their work contributes to the bigger picture, they feel a deeper sense of purpose and commitment.

- **Managerial Influence: The Impact of Direct Supervisors on Engagement** - Your manager isn't just a boss; they're a crucial link to your engagement. A supportive manager who communicates openly, provides feedback, and shows genuine interest in your growth can make all the difference in how engaged you feel at work.

- **Alignment of Personal and Organizational Goals** - When your goals align with the company's objectives, work feels meaningful. It's about knowing how your individual efforts contribute to the organization's success and feeling motivated to achieve those shared goals.

- **Transparency and Communication: Keeping Employees Informed and Involved** - Openness and transparency build trust. Employees want to be kept in the loop about what's happening in the company, whether it's good news or challenges. Feeling informed and involved makes them feel valued and part of the team.

- **Impact of Organizational Changes on Engagement** - Change is constant, but how it's managed affects engagement. Whether it's a merger, restructuring, or new technology, involving employees in the process and addressing their concerns helps maintain morale and engagement during transitions.

- **Technology and Engagement** - In today's digital age, technology isn't just a tool; it's a bridge that connects teams, facilitates communication, and supports collaboration. Leveraging technology effectively can enhance engagement, especially in remote or hybrid work settings.

- **Feedback Mechanisms** - Feedback isn't just about performance reviews; it's about listening to employees' ideas, concerns, and suggestions. Creating regular feedback loops shows employees their voices matter and helps improve engagement by addressing their needs.

- **Learning and Development** - Opportunities for growth and development aren't perks; they're essential for engagement. Investing in employees' skills and career progression shows a commitment to their future within the organization, boosting motivation and loyalty.

- **Flexibility and Adaptability** - Work-life balance isn't a luxury; it's a necessity for engagement. Flexible work arrangements and supportive policies that accommodate diverse needs promote well-being and allow employees to perform at their best.

- **Community and Social Responsibility** - Engaged employees care about more than just their jobs; they want to make a positive impact. Involvement in community initiatives and corporate social responsibility efforts not only enhances engagement but also strengthens the company's reputation.

- **Health and Well-being Initiatives** - Supporting employee well-being isn't just about physical health; it's about mental and emotional wellness too. Initiatives like wellness programs and mental health support demonstrate a commitment to employees' holistic well-being.

- **Recognition Beyond Rewards** - Recognition isn't just about bonuses; it's about feeling valued and appreciated. Acknowledging contributions through praise, opportunities for growth, and celebrating achievements fosters a culture where employees feel recognized and motivated.

By focusing on these often-overlooked aspects of employee engagement, organizations can create a workplace where employees are not only productive but also passionate about their work and committed to the company's success.

Developing an Action Plan

> *"Success is not final, failure is not fatal: It is the courage to continue that counts."*
> *– Winston Churchill*

In the journey towards fostering a highly engaged workforce, developing a robust action plan is key to translating intentions into impactful results. How can leaders effectively assess, strategize, and implement initiatives that enhance employee engagement? Let's delve into actionable steps:

Assessing Current Engagement Levels: Tools and Techniques

- **Start with a Baseline:** Begin by utilizing employee surveys, feedback sessions, and engagement metrics to understand current levels of engagement.

- **Gather Insights:** Analyze data to identify strengths, areas for improvement, and potential barriers to engagement.

- **Use Tools Wisely:** Employ tools like pulse surveys, focus groups, and one-on-one discussions to gather qualitative insights alongside quantitative data.

Setting SMART Goals for Improvement

- **Specific Objectives:** Define clear and specific goals that address identified gaps in engagement.

- **Measurable Outcomes:** Establish metrics and benchmarks to track progress and measure success.

- **Achievable Targets:** Set realistic goals that are challenging yet attainable within the organization's resources and timeline.

- **Relevant Initiatives:** Align goals with organizational priorities and employee needs.

- **Time-Bound Deadlines:** Establish timelines for achieving milestones and completing action steps.

Implementing Strategies: From Theory to Practice

- **Communication and Transparency:** Ensure clear communication of the action plan, goals, and expected outcomes to all stakeholders.

- **Leadership Buy-In:** Secure commitment and support from senior leaders to drive implementation and overcome resistance.

- **Employee Involvement:** Involve employees in the process by soliciting feedback, co-creating solutions, and fostering ownership.

- **Allocate Resources:** Allocate necessary resources, including time, budget, and personnel, to support engagement initiatives.

Monitoring Progress and Adjusting Strategies as Needed

- **Regular Evaluation:** Continuously monitor engagement metrics and feedback loops to assess progress.

- **Flexibility and Adaptability:** Remain agile in adjusting strategies based on evolving feedback and changing organizational dynamics.

- **Celebrate Successes:** Recognize and celebrate achievements and milestones to sustain momentum and morale.

Developing an effective action plan requires a blend of strategic foresight, genuine commitment, and proactive execution. By systematically assessing, setting SMART goals, implementing strategies, and monitoring progress, organizations can foster a culture of high employee engagement that drives sustainable success and organizational resilience.

Fostering Employee Engagement for Organizational Success

Throughout this chapter, we've explored the transformative power of employee engagement—a cornerstone for organizational success in today's dynamic workplaces. We've debunked myths, examined key metrics, and highlighted strategies that go beyond traditional approaches to foster a deeply engaged workforce.

From creating a culture of trust and open communication to empowering employees through growth opportunities and recognition programs, we've uncovered essential tactics that leaders can implement. We've emphasized the critical role of leadership in setting the tone, aligning goals, and championing transparency to drive engagement and performance.

Additionally, we've discussed often-overlooked factors such as emotional connection to the organization's mission, the influence of direct supervisors, and the impact of organizational changes on engagement levels. These insights underscore the holistic approach needed to sustain high levels of engagement.

Charge: Taking Action for Lasting Impact

Imagine a workplace where employees don't just clock in and out but are genuinely excited to contribute to something bigger. Employee engagement is the secret ingredient that turns this vision into reality. It's about creating a space where every team member feels valued, motivated, and connected to the organization's mission. When engagement is high, employees are not just satisfied—they are driven by purpose and passion, leading to increased productivity, innovation, and overall success.

As leaders, it's your role to nurture this environment by actively listening, recognizing contributions, and fostering a culture of growth and inclusivity. By embracing these principles, you're not only enhancing individual performance but also driving your organization towards a future of excellence and resilience. Remember, the power of engagement lies in the meaningful connections you build and the opportunities you create for your team to thrive.

> **REFLECTION AND APPLICATION**
>
> - How would you assess the current level of employee engagement within your team or organization? What indicators or feedback mechanisms have you used to gauge engagement effectively?
> - Considering the strategies discussed, what specific SMART goals could you set to enhance employee engagement in your workplace? How might these goals align with broader organizational objectives?
> - Which of the strategies outlined—such as fostering a culture of trust, enhancing recognition programs, or promoting work-life balance—do you believe could have the most significant impact in your context? What steps will you take to implement these strategies effectively?

CHAPTER 15

THE NEED FOR OUTSIDE PERSPECTIVE

> *"There is only one way to look at things until someone shows us how to look at them with different eyes."*
>
> ~ Pablo Picasso

In This Chapter

- When you Need a DEIB Consultant
- Questions to Ask Before Hiring a DEIB Consultant
- Working with Your DEIB Consultant
- Reflection and Application

So, maybe by now you have decided that the DEIB effort is worth it. Yet, you are not convinced you need or have the budget for a DEIB consultant. Of course, I am biased and would tell you everyone needs a DEIB consultant. However, I will not try to convince you if you are not ready. Instead, I have offered all the *get you started* type of information and tips I can. Perhaps, you want a DEIB expert, but the budget just isn't there yet. That's okay. I'm in it for the long haul. So, let me give you all the ammunition you need to argue the case for a DEIB expert coming on board. When you need one, questions to ask, and even what to expect when working with one.

Remember, having a DEIB expert is about providing an outside perspective and helping you work through the cultural bias you have but may not recognize.

When You Need A DEIB Expert

Sometimes it's hard to tell if you can do it without an expert. However, if you feel like you need help or missed the bus on the following, you might want to consider an expert:

- You need help refining your organization's DEIB goals
- You need help evaluating and assessing your organization's DEIB efforts
- The organization's current efforts aren't improving the culture
- The organization doesn't understand the DEIB lingo
- You did diversity training one time, and it didn't work
- There's been an *incident*

Of course, there are several other reasons you may need an expert. For now, let's focus on the big ones.

First, you may not know how to incorporate and refine DEIB into your organizational goals. DEIB can weave into HR goals of hiring and retention or employee satisfaction. Further, DEIB objectives could help boost productivity and the bottom line. It's about seeing how they are interconnected and working one into the other.

Second, it's about seeing things from a different perspective. Evaluating and assessing your DEIB future plans and the current effort is essential for success. What you think is working may not be so. Think about it this way — have you ever sat at your desk and pulled your hair out trying to figure out why your computer wouldn't turn on? You call your tech support and wait for them to show up only to find out the computer somehow got unplugged from the wall? You were too close and couldn't see the smaller details because you looked at the big picture. This is like that!

Third, maybe you have DEIB initiatives in place but struggle to see improvement. You have unwilling participants, or your training and engagement efforts are resented. You believe you are doing everything by the book, but your DEIB isn't clicking for some reason. It very well could be that you put the cart before the horse in some places. DEIB isn't built in a day and needs to start with that solid ground and foundation, remember?

Maybe you do an annual DEIB or 'sensitivity' training and find it pointless. Well, hopefully, by now, you see it is. However, you aren't sure what to do, what it will cost, and whether everyone will accept it.

Worse yet, and often why DEIB experts are called in—the incident. More often than not, the expert is called in to help clean up a mess. It could be the cultural acceptance of a particular language or words or a significant incident like a hate crime that took place and made its way to the media.

Finally, if you find that you have been put on notice for your lack of understanding of current language or DEIB lingo, it might be time to call in the expert. The DEIB world and the language change frequently. Heck, maybe you didn't even realize you are still stuck at the equity level and haven't made it to inclusion and belonging. I know it can be an eye-opener!

So, you know more now than you did, but you still aren't sure you need an expert. Well, there are some questions you should be asking at the organizational level before you hire a DEIB consultant.

Ask Before Hiring

Consider the following five questions:[56]

- Does the organization have a DEIB Strategic Plan?
- Are you looking for compliance or proactive education? (compliance = lawsuit avoidance)
- Are trainings required or voluntary?
- What is the culture and context of your organization? Meaning, what is the organizational level of DEIB understanding?
- What is the social identity of the consultant? Who will the DEIB message be best received from? For example, if you have a dominant white male workforce, will they best receive the DEIB message from another white male, or would they be receptive to a BIPOC consultant?

---

[56] https://www.denasamuels.com/5-things-to-consider-when-youre-hiring-a-diversity-inclusiveness-consultant/

Finally, have you done any research—surveys, listening sessions, focus groups, etc.? That baseline is essential and can be time-consuming.

When It's Go Time

Are you finally convinced it's time to hire an expert?! If so, there are a few things to keep in mind.

When you have hired the expert (hopefully with executive sponsorship), it's time to establish that working relationship with leaders so DEIB can be embedded into your organizational DNA. You should see your DEIB expert as a partner and introduce the relationship as that. You then want to bring others into the process immediately. The more, the merrier! This means the board, senior leaders, managers, HR, and even employees or staff from different levels.

The more engaged people, the better the ground and foundation will be. You will work to create groups to gather information, create surveys, and work to understand employees' concerns. It is about gaining insight, learning about the culture, and establishing a baseline to work from. You will also work to figure out what the organization is looking to achieve and what the workforce needs or wants. Finally, you can clarify the levels of commitment for the top down and bottom up.

From there, you work to identify the project scope and establish a budget. Often, the two go hand in hand. You want to know what is included in the partnership you create. Will the project involve developing a DEIB strategy that works with the organizational business plan? Will it include training? If so, how much and what type? What about change management and labor relations? Finally, will you want the project to include talent management and development? Of course, this isn't an all-inclusive list of what a project can cover. Every organization has different needs. But you get the point. And sometimes, it comes down to budget, and a more extensive engagement might need to be dissected into smaller projects that can fit within budget requirements.

That brings us to defining the length of the engagement. First, consider if you want a long-term partnership or if you want to engage an expert on a project basis. Every consultant is different; some have precise processes, expertise, training, and approaches. All of which could determine the length and type of engagement.

Finally, while it goes without saying, you should take the time to vet your DEIB expert carefully. Do they only offer canned DEIB solutions? Or are they problem solvers that work to deliver custom solutions for your organizational needs? How do you know?

As with anything, ask. Ask for referrals, ask for credentials, and review their certifications, education, and accomplishments. Of course, you may have to think more broadly and keep an open mind. This is because the education, training, and experience DEIB experts have can be far and wide. For example, one might have a degree in business while another may have a degree in behavioral sciences. Maybe one is a retired attorney, and another worked for the NAACP before branching out.

The key to remember is that DEIB is a very broad scope of expertise, and you want to be comfortable with the expert you choose to work with. Most selection processes come down to choosing someone you think will fit within the organization. In this case, you should seriously consider the one who makes you slightly uncomfortable.

The DEIB expert you choose should challenge you. You don't want someone telling you how right you are. Most often, it is the tough love you need—the reality check. You need borderline brutally honest mixed with optimism.

> **REFLECTION AND APPLICATION**
>
> - What is prompting your need for a DEIB expert?
> - Do you know what you want to accomplish by partnering with a DEIB expert?
> - What characteristics, expertise, or experience do you feel is essential in a DEIB expert?

ABOUT THE AUTHOR

T. Renee' Smith is the CEO of iSuccess Consulting, Inc., a global consulting firm dedicated to cultivating DEIB ecosystems within corporations, government entities, nonprofit organizations, and small to medium-sized businesses.

With nearly 30 years of experience in DEIB, Ms. Smith has worked with major corporations like Delta Air Lines and government agencies such as the General Services Administration (GSA), specializing in DEIB and Supplier Diversity. Often finding herself as the sole person of color or one of few in boardroom discussions, Ms. Smith brings a unique perspective to the table.

From her early years as a page for the Honorable Congressman John Lewis at just 14 years old, where she stood out as one of the few pages of color and women among hundreds, to her academic and professional journey at Georgia State University, and internships with Coca-Cola Enterprises and AT&T, Ms. Smith has confronted exclusion, discrimination, and marginalization.

Married to a veteran, with a youngest son who is Nerodiverse, a sister with multiple sclerosis, and a niece who is part of the LGBTQI+ community, Ms. Smith's lived experiences drive her determination to challenge the status quo, advocate for equitable representation, and dismantle systems perpetuating inequity.

Throughout her career, Ms. Smith has encountered instances where her business was the most qualified and experienced but overlooked due to contracts being awarded to businesses with established connections and networks. Despite these challenges, she remains committed to changing the narrative, promoting common ground, and emphasizing our shared humanity through DEIB initiatives.

DEIB is not just a professional pursuit for Ms. Smith; it is deeply ingrained in her journey, history, and passion. She continues to use her experiences as opportunities for education, empowerment, and bridge-building in diverse communities and workplaces.

iSuccess Business Model

iSuccess empowers organizations to achieve inclusive excellence by helping them solve complex DEIB people and supplier challenges using real-time data, experiential learning, and an innovative lab approach grounded in human-centered design. We have extensive experience setting and executing DEIB strategy, improving client experience, and attracting and developing diverse talent. Equally important, we have a passion for business inclusion and empowerment.

> When we listen and celebrate what is both common and different, we become wiser, more inclusive, and better as an organization.
>
> — **Pat Wadors**

If you enjoyed reading Beyond Differences:
How Great Leaders Build Bridges, Drive Change,
and Sustain Impact
Please leave us a review!

Connect with iSuccess on social media:
@iSuccessConsult
www.isuccessconsulting.com

Made in the USA
Middletown, DE
25 August 2024